Do Hummingbirds Hum?

Animal Q&A: Fascinating Answers to Questions about Animals

Animal Q&A books invite readers to explore the secret lives of animals. Covering everything from their basic biology to their complex behaviors at every stage of life to issues in conservation, these richly illustrated books provide detailed information in an accessible style that brings to life the science and natural history of a variety of species.

Do Butterflies Bite? Fascinating Answers to Questions about Butterflies and Moths by Hazel Davies and Carol A. Butler

Do Bats Drink Blood? Fascinating Answers to Questions about Bats, by Barbara A. Schmidt-French and Carol A. Butler

Why Do Bees Buzz? Fascinating Answers to Questions about Bees, by Elizabeth Capaldi Evans and Carol A. Butler

Do Hummingbirds Hum?

Fascinating Answers to Questions about Hummingbirds

George C. West
and Carol A. Butler

Rutgers University Press
NEW BRUNSWICK, NEW JERSEY, AND LONDON

Library of Congress Cataloging-in-Publication Data

West, George C.
  Do hummingbirds hum? : fascinating answers to questions about hummingbirds / George C. West and Carol A. Butler.
    p. cm. — (Animal Q & A)
  Includes bibliographical references and index.
  ISBN 978-0-8135-4738-1 (pbk. : alk. paper)
  1. Hummingbirds—Miscellanea. I. Butler, Carol A., 1943– II. Title.
  QL696.A558W47 2010
  598.7'64—dc22

                  2009049511

A British Cataloging-in-Publication record for this book is available from the British Library.

Black-and-white illustrations and photographs are by George C. West, unless otherwise noted.

Visit our Web site: http://rutgerspress.rutgers.edu

Manufactured in the United States of America

Contents

THREE Feathers and Bones   50

FOUR Reproduction   69

Appendices

A color insert follows page 94

Preface

Of all animated beings [hummingbirds are] the most elegant in form and brilliant in color. The stones and metals polished by art are not comparable to this gem of nature. She has placed it in the order of birds, but among the tiniest of the race; . . . she has loaded it with all the gifts of which she has only given other birds a share.

—Georges-Louis Leclerc, Comte du Buffon,
French naturalist and artist (1707–1788)

In the 1700s when an interest in nature often meant killing your subject, hummingbirds were skinned, stuffed, and studied. A variety of drawings and paintings based on their stuffed skins attempted to catalogue their fabulous variety, and their skins were made into amulets, articles of clothing, artificial flowers, and other ornaments so that people could possess their beauty. Today, the interest on the part of birders and amateur naturalists in hummingbirds seems to rival or even outstrip the interest in butterflies, perhaps because like butterflies they are both beautiful and accessible.

This book, the fourth on important pollinators, continues in the style of the comprehensive *Do Butterflies Bite?* It provides an overview of hummingbird biology for the general reader, and more detailed discussions of hummingbird morphology and behavior for the reader who wants to go beyond the basics. We also have included a wide range of information for people interested in attracting, photographing, and observing hummingbirds in the wild or in captivity, as well as details about banding and a discussion of conservation issues. Because of hummingbirds' small size, amazing flight abilities, and relative accessibility, many scientists actively study them in the laboratory and the field. We have included a substantial amount of the fascinating results of their research to enrich our answers.

We have maintained the tone of the series by writing in a non-technical, friendly style, defining scientific terms as we go along. Carol A. Butler with Hazel Davies initiated this series of question-and-answer books based on their experience answering all sorts of questions about butterflies in the live butterfly exhibit at New York's American Museum of Natural History. George West was an excellent choice to co-author this book, because he has been answering questions about birds for many years. His former position as a research professor at the University of Alaska Fairbanks, where he studied the physiology and ecology of arctic and subarctic birds, along with his lifetime interest in birding, have made him exceptionally well informed.

Over the past seven years, George has processed more than fourteen thousand hummingbirds in southeastern Arizona as part of research conducted by the Hummingbird Monitoring Network (HMN). HMN is a science-based, project-driven, non-profit organization dedicated to the conservation of hummingbird diversity and abundance throughout the Americas, and the purpose of their research is to determine which areas are the most important for hummingbird survival. Every other Monday from March to October, George sets up a banding station at an altitude of 5300 feet on private land in Madera Canyon within the Coronado National Forest in the Santa Rita Mountains south of Tucson, Arizona. For five hours beginning at sunrise, he traps, quickly processes, and releases all the hummingbirds that come to his feeders. Assisted by his wife Ellen and a group of volunteers, and on one occasion by co-author Carol Butler, George examines each bird in the order in which it was captured, recording the time, species, sex, and life stage of the bird. He measures its wing, tail, and bill, checks for molt, weighs the bird, and examines its abdomen for signs of migratory fat or for evidence of an egg within. If the bird is already wearing a band, its number is recorded; if not, George applies a tiny, uniquely numbered band to its right leg. Then he refreshes the bird with a drink of nectar and releases it. We have included a series of questions and answers about banding that explain and illustrate the process in greater depth.

We think you will find that this book answers most of your questions about hummingbirds. It also contains lots of interesting facts that apply to birds in general and some photographs and drawings to give you an idea of the color and form of these beautiful little birds. In the event that you have questions that we do not answer or if you want to see more birds, we have provided a list of additional readings and web sites that are rich resources for specific information and images. We hope you enjoy reading this book as much as we have enjoyed writing it.

Acknowledgments

From GW: It was an honor to be selected as the coauthor of this book, which answers the many questions we are asked while operating a public hummingbird-banding station in Madera Canyon, Arizona. It was a pleasure working with a tireless coauthor, Carol Butler, in bringing this information to a public who enjoys one of nature's masterpieces, the hummingbird. The more we learn about a group of birds, the more diligent we become about preserving and protecting them and their habitat. Thanks to Susan Wethington, executive director of the Hummingbird Monitoring Network, for reviewing the first draft of the entire text and to Holly Ernest, research veterinarian from the University of California, Davis, for providing insights into the diseases and parasites with which hummingbirds might be afflicted. Jim Burns, Arthur Grosset, Bill Maynard, David Southall, and Allen Tozier very generously allowed us to use some of their magnificent photographs in this book for which we are very grateful.

I have been banding birds since 1960, but Ruth Russell, hummingbird bander from Tucson, Arizona, kindly trained me to band hummingbirds. Luis and Nancy Calvo in Madera Canyon, Tom and Edith Beatty in Miller Canyon, and Melva Robin in Arivaca, Arizona, served as site hosts for our monitoring program and we greatly appreciate their support. I appreciate the great patience my wife, Ellen, has for my work at the computer writing and illustrating and for her dedication to the hummingbird-monitoring research program. Without her help, this might be possible, but certainly not as enjoyable.

From CB: My thanks to George West and his wife Ellen for their kindness and hospitality when I visited Arizona to observe and assist George in banding hummingbirds, and to George for his good-humored enthusiasm about this book. My continued appreciation to my agent Deirdre Mullane for her guidance and encouragement, and to Doreen Valentine and the Rutgers University Press staff for their support and input. We also are grateful to Bobbe Needham for her sensitive and intelligent copyediting, and to my daughter Aisha for doing the index. I am also indebted to the people who exhibit and breed hummingbirds—they shared their personal knowledge with me to supplement the limited published information that is available about hummingbirds in captivity. Thanks to Karen Krebbs from the Arizona-Sonora Desert Museum, Ron Boender of Butterfly World, Ken Reininger at the North Carolina Zoo, and the Dutch contingent, who are always wonderfully forthcoming and generous with their time. Ko Veltman, Ton Hilhorst, Hans Bontenbal, and Rob Gase of Artis Royal Zoo enthusiastically took me to visit their new hummingbirds, as did Joost Lammers from Vogelpark Avifauna. Pierre de Wit from Zoo Emmen, hummingbird breeder Jack Rovers, and Menno Schilthuizen from Naturalis were also very supportive and helpful. I am grateful to the others who contributed bits and pieces, answered questions, and furthered my understanding of these beautiful little birds. Everyone, and especially George, made this project possible and enjoyable.

Do Hummingbirds Hum?

ONE

Hummingbird Basics

Question 1: What is a hummingbird?

Answer: Hummingbirds are the smallest birds in the world. They are incredibly maneuverable, spectacularly fast-flying birds that are often brilliantly colored. Although they vary from species to species, most people think of them as tiny, iridescent birds with long bills and an amazing ability to hover. This describes some male hummingbirds, but many species are quite plain, as are the females of most species where the male is colorful.

Their unsurpassed ability to hover like a bee at a flower or a feeder makes them accessible and fascinating backyard birds to observe. They can stop and start in the air, and they fly backward as well as up, down, and sideways. Ospreys, kestrels, Rough-legged Hawks, kingfishers, and most passerine birds (such as warblers) can hover very briefly, but no other bird has a hummingbird's ability to hover for prolonged periods. This ability also makes hummingbirds efficient pollinators of 129 types of plants in the United States, according to the most complete figures we could find reported by Verne Grant, a renowned Canadian expert on plant speciation. They also pollinate at least 58 families of plants in Brazil, according to Josep del Hoyo and his colleagues in *Handbook of the Birds of the World*. Their size (from tip of bill to end of tail) ranges from only about 2 inches (5 centimeters) to about 8¾ inches (22 centimeters). Species with long streamer tails can be up to 14 inches in length (35 centimeters). Their plumage is often strikingly iridescent, and many species

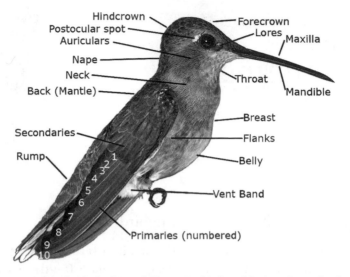

Figure 1. A female Black-chinned Hummingbird *Archilochus alexandri,* showing the features of external anatomy and primary flight feathers.

have a brightly colored gorget (throat patch), crown, and/or tail. They may have elongated or modified tail feathers, puff-feathered thighs, or extended gorget feathers that are unlike the plumage of any other birds. The bill of a hummingbird is characteristically very thin, enabling it to easily probe flowers for nectar. Depending on the flowers a bird feeds from, the bill may be very short or extremely long, and it may be straight or deeply curved.

Question 2: How do hummingbirds differ from other birds?

Answer: Almost all hummingbirds are smaller than other birds, and the smaller species are the smallest of all birds. However, some species of hummingbird are more than four inches in total body length and therefore are similar in size to familiar birds like flycatchers, chickadees, wrens, warblers, sparrows, and finches. Hummingbirds are proportionally different from other birds because the head is large in relation to the rest of the body in order to accommodate a large brain, one of the largest of all birds with respect to their body size (see Chapter 2, Question 1: Are hummingbirds intelligent?).

Hummingbirds are the only birds that can truly hover, in part because their wing bones are proportionately different from those of most other birds; the humerus (upper arm bone) and the fused radius and ulna (arm bones below the equivalent of the human elbow) are very short, while the carpals (wrist bones), metacarpals, and phalanges (hand bones) are very long. The joint between the coracoid and the sternum is unique to hummingbirds and swifts, which are considered by most experts to be in the same order, Apodiformes (meaning "no feet"). This unique wing support structure gives hummingbirds the ability to orient their wings in almost any direction.

Question 3: Where in the world are hummingbirds found?

Answer: Native Americans gave some of the Pilgrims hummingbird earrings. Soldiers and missionaries in Mexico encountered Aztec kings who wore cloaks made entirely of hummingbird skins. By the middle of the nineteenth century, hundreds of thousands of hummingbirds were being killed in South America and shipped to London and other cities in Europe, where the skins were purchased for collections and for making artificial flowers and other ornaments. Serious interest in these tiny birds grew, and between 1829 and 1832, René P. Lesson published a three-volume monograph, illustrated with color plates, about hummingbirds. Between 1849 and 1861, John Gould, a talented English taxidermist with no formal university training, published a five-volume monograph containing 360 hand-colored lithographic plates of hummingbirds copied from stuffed skins. Gould traveled to the United States and saw his first live hummingbirds in 1857.

Hummingbirds are found only in North, Central, and South America, including the Caribbean islands. They are predominantly tropical and subtropical birds, with the greatest number

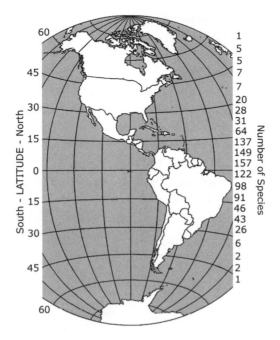

Figure 2. Distribution of hummingbirds by latitude. Numbers represent counts of species per five-degree latitude increment. Species with a wide latitudinal distribution are recorded at several latitudes on the map. (*Illustration based on data from* Clements Checklist of Birds of the World)

of species found within ten degrees north and south of the equator. The farther from the equator one travels, the fewer species of hummingbirds one will find (see figure 2). For example, Ecuador, a country the size of Colorado that is on the equator, has more than 125 species, whereas Colorado has only 4 regularly occurring species.

Different species have adapted to different climates, life zones with a particular range of temperature and humidity in which they thrive. These zones occur at different altitudes in regions that range from the southern tip of Chile to the equator and north to Alaska. A few species can even tolerate snow and cold, and a few others thrive in the high temperatures and low humidity of the desert. Most species live in forests, with the highest number residing in tropical montane forests (evergreen mountain forests where clouds and mist are regularly in contact with the forest vegetation), and at lower elevations in submontane forests.

In South America, a few species live all year at elevations above 4,000 meters (13,000 feet) in the Andes Mountains. At that altitude, they face little competition for the abundant flowers and insect life at the margin of glaciers and snow patches. There are more species lower down in the wet mountain meadows, which are covered with flowering herbaceous plants that are rich in nectar. The drier areas of the mountains are less attractive to hummingbirds, and few species live there. More species can be found along the edges of the forest and in scattered brush vegetation surrounded by grassland. There is greater species diversity in the montane forests between 3,500 and 1,800 meters (11,500 and 5,900 feet), which host a variety of flowering trees, vines, shrubs, and flowers. From 1,500 meters (4,900 feet) to sea level, the number of species and abundance of hummingbirds decrease as the variety of vegetation decreases.

Western North America has more varied habitat than does the east coast. The hummingbirds' habitat in Mexico, as well as their overland migration routes in that country, probably

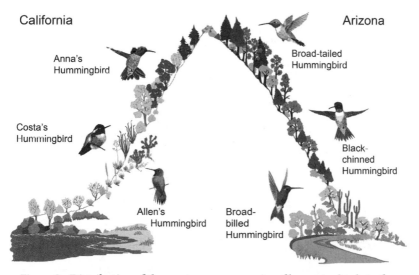

Figure 3. Distribution of the most common species of hummingbirds in the sky islands of Arizona and the coastal mountains of California.

Hummingbirds Found on Some of the Caribbean Islands

Antigua	Antillean Crested, Green-throated Carib, Purple-throated Carib
Aruba	Blue-tailed Emerald
Bahamas	Cuban Emerald, Bahama Woodstar, Ruby-throated
Barbados	Antillean Crested, Purple-throated Carib, Green-throated Carib
Barbuda	Antillean Crested, Green-throated Carib
Cuba	Cuban Emerald, Bee, Ruby-throated
Curaçao	Blue-tailed Emerald
Dominica	Antillean Crested, Blue-headed, Purple-throated Carib
Grenada	Rufous-breasted Hermit, Green-throated Carib, Antillean Crested, Purple-throated Carib
Hispaniola	Antillean Mango, Hispaniolan Emerald, Vervain
Jamaica	Jamaican Mango, Western (Red-billed) Streamertail, Eastern (Black-billed) Streamertail, Vervain
Martinique	Blue-headed, Green-breasted Mango, Antillean Crested, Green-throated Carib, Purple-throated Carib
Puerto Rico	Antillean Mango, Green Mango, Green-throated Carib, Antillean Crested, Puerto Rican Emerald
St. Lucia	Antillean Crested, Purple-throated Carib
St.Vincents	Antillean Crested, Blue-headed, Green-throated Carib, Purple-throated Carib
Tobago	Rufous-breasted Hermit, White-necked Jacobin, Black-throated Mango, Ruby-topaz, Blue-chinned Sapphire, Copper-rumped, White-tailed Sabrewing

Hummingbirds Found on Some of the Caribbean Islands

Trinidad	Rufous-breasted Hermit, Green Hermit, Little Hermit, White-necked Jacobin, Brown Violet-ear, Black-throated Mango, Green-throated Mango, Ruby-topaz, Tufted Coquette, Blue-chinned Sapphire, Blue-tailed Emerald, White-chested Emerald, Copper-rumped
Virgin Islands	Antillean Mango, Purple-throated Carib, Green-throated Carib, Antillean Crested

account for the evolution of many diverse species within the approximately seventeen genera that are commonly found near the northern Mexican border. Hybrids have been observed by many birders and banders. Most are the result of crossbreeding between species belonging to different genera (see Chapter 4, Question 5: Can hummingbirds of one species mate with those of another species?).

Question 4: How did hummingbirds evolve?

Answer: It is difficult to be specific about the history of hummingbirds because our understanding of their evolution is steadily improving. Following a framework published by Robert Bleiweiss and colleagues in 1997 and 1998, Jimmy McGuire at the University of California at Riverside and colleagues compared gene sequences of 151 of the more than 335 hummingbird species. They propose a reevaluation of the evolutionary relationships among the most basic taxonomic groups or clades. A clade is a group with a single common ancestor that includes all the descendants of that ancestor. The researchers concluded that "most of the principal clades of hummingbirds (all but

Co-adaptation

Most scientists believe that the method of pollen dispersal from one flower to another evolved along with the pollinating organism to the mutual benefit of the plant and the pollinator.

The great variety in the length and degree of curvature of hummingbird bills evolved, for example, as certain flowering plants developed attributes that heightened their attractiveness to hummingbird pollinators. This process is known as co-adaptation or co-evolution. The result of this process of natural selection is that hummingbirds and plants developed shapes that fit together, so that the bird could rely on the flower for nectar, and the flower could rely on the bird for pollination.

This theory suggests that when a species is the sole pollinator of a flower, and that species disappears from the habitat, the plants that relied on it would reach an evolutionary dead end and disappear. New research has challenged this concept, suggesting that some specialized plants may have more evolutionary flexibility than had been thought. Erin Tripp and Paul Manos at Duke University studied pollination in 115 species of flowers of the genus *Ruella*. Using DNA sampling, they statistically reconstructed the likely evolutionary development and ancestry of the contemporary *Ruella* species. They found that flower shape and color were generally a good fit with the pollinators that served the particular species, but it appeared that between eight and eleven plants had made a transition from hummingbirds to insects as their preferred pollinators. This may have occurred because the plants were originally in areas where hummingbirds were populous, then dispersed to habitats without hummingbirds.

There is some interesting research on plants that are fertilized by more than one pollinator. Focused on the interaction and success of various combinations, Robert Berlin studied pollination of the same flowers at four sites in Illinois and Missouri.

Co-adaptation

The flower, the trumpet creeper (*Campsis radicans* of the family Bignoniaceae), is pollinated by hummingbirds as well as by two species of bees. Only 1 to 9 percent of the flowers produced mature fruits at the four sites, and he found that compared to honey bees and bumblebees, Ruby-throated Hummingbirds deposited ten times as much pollen on a stigma (the tip of the flower's ovary) per visit, and flowers produced fruit more frequently where hummingbirds were the most frequent visitors.

John Pleasants of Iowa State University and Nickolas Waser of University of California, Riverside, studied the curious phenomenon of bumblebees that, during a short period in 1981, were observed actively foraging at *Ipomopsis* flowers usually visited only by hummingbirds. For many reasons, these flowers are normally not inviting to bees: they have deep corollas that exceed the length of the bumblebee proboscis, so the bee cannot reach the nectar; they have no scent, and bees use odor as a nectar guide; the shape of the flower does not provide a lip for the bees to land on—not a problem for a hovering hummingbird; and the flowers are red, a color that is not known to attract bees. In 1981 for a few short weeks, these flowers averaged an unusually high amount of nectar due to environmental conditions, so the nectar was easier for the bumblebees to reach. These observations demonstrate that bumblebees, which sample a variety of plants in their habitat, will pollinate new varieties if there is a profitable nectar reward. We get a glimpse with this interesting example of how over time plants may convert from one pollinator to another when environmental conditions produce sustained changes in plant morphology.

Hummingbirds also tend to seek out new food sources, according to University of Texas botanist Verne Grant, who suggests that plants he studied (in the Arcto-Tertiary plant group) that converted at some point in their history from bee

(continued)

Co-adaptation, *continued*

or butterfly to hummingbird pollination may have done so because these plants grew alongside flowers that were already being pollinated by hummingbirds. When the hummingbirds proved a reliable pollinator for the plants, they evolved flowers that were a better fit for the hummingbirds than for their prior pollinators. It seems apparent that the evolutionary relationship between plants and pollinators should not be oversimplified, even though basic adaptation does occur.

Mountain Gems and possibly Bee Hummingbirds) originated in the lowlands of South America. Their research demonstrated that there have been at least thirty independent invasions by groups of hummingbirds, most to Central America and some to other primary landmasses.

Modern birds are thought to have appeared during the Cretaceous era, more than sixty-five million years ago (mya). Scientists agree that birds radiated or spread out geographically throughout the Paleocene era (thirty-seven to sixty-five mya), prior to the separation of the continents as we know them today, and it is likely that during this period the ancestors of today's hummingbirds appeared in the Americas. Very few hummingbird fossil remains have been found because their tiny bones disintegrate before they have a chance to fossilize. Robert Bleiweiss and his colleagues believe, based on DNA analysis of approximately 25 percent of hummingbird genera, that most of the radiation of extant hummingbirds from South America took place during the uplifting of the northern part of the Andes mountains between twelve and thirteen mya.

Hummingbirds are continuing to evolve, as reported by Jaime Garcia-Moreno and colleagues at the Max Planck Institute for Ornithology in Radolfzell, Germany. Areas north and south of the Isthmus of Panama are rich in diversity of hummingbirds due to frequent speciation before the uprising of the land bridge that joined South and Central America. The researchers' DNA studies show that one genus, *Lampornis*, originated before the uprising of the land, and subsequent speciation has occurred that may place some species in a different genus.

Until recently, the oldest hummingbird fossils on record, found in a cave in Central America, were dated at between one and two million years old. But in 2004, Gerald Mayr of the Senckenberg Museum in Germany identified fossil remains of skeletons less than two inches (five centimeters) long that had been found in a clay deposit in southwestern Germany, the first bones of hummingbird-like fossils ever found outside the Americas. He wryly named the new species *Eurotrochilus inexpectatus*, which translates as "an unexpected European version of *Trochilus*." (*Trochilus* is a modern hummingbird genus.) The newly discovered fossils have been dated thirty-four to thirty million years ago, and the fossilized skull and bill make it clear that they differ from swifts that presently share the order Apodiformes with hummingbirds (see this chapter, Question 5: How are hummingbirds classified?). In 2007, there was a report that a similar fossil (*Eurotrochilus sp.*), originally found in Provence, France, in the 1980s, was rediscovered by Antoine Louchart in a colleague's private collection. Louchart is presently a researcher at the Ecole Normale Supérieure et Université de Lyon in France. The fossil he brought to light is described as well preserved, with its vertebrae and the bones of its feet intact. In 2008, there was a report of a hummingbird fossil found in Poland that has a bone supporting the shoulder muscles (the coracoid) that resembles a similar bone observed in swifts. This specimen is generally similar to that of the German fossil, but it is described as a new species of the same genus.

Douglas Altshuler at the University of California, Riverside, and Robert Dudley of the Smithsonian Tropical Research Institute in Panama suggest that as hummingbirds evolved, they moved to higher-elevation habitats that are associated with adaptive changes in wing-beat patterns, increased body mass, and larger wing area. Although the emphasis in studies of their evolution has been on the behaviors developed to obtain nectar from flowers, these researchers suggest that flight behaviors involved in competing and foraging for insects may also have influenced the evolution of the variety of hummingbird body and wing sizes and shapes.

Question 5: How are hummingbirds classified?

Answer: Hummingbirds belong to the class Aves (birds), all of whose members are feathered vertebrates with a four-chambered heart that lay eggs. They are in the order Apodiformes, birds with small feet, highly developed flight ability, short upper wing bones, and a unique shoulder joint. They have eight pairs of ribs, while most birds have only six. They have an elongated and deeply keeled sternum to contain the two greatly enlarged thoracic muscles that power the wings. The combined weight of these muscles can be up to 30 percent of the bird's body weight.

The name Apodiformes literally means the order of birds with no feet. Obviously hummingbirds do have feet, but early biologists must have thought that the feet of birds in this group were so small that they were relatively useless, and in fact all hummingbirds have tiny feet used only to perch and not to walk or run. The order Apodiformes contains three families: Hemiprocnidae, the treeswifts; Apodidae, the true swifts; and Trochilidae, the hummingbirds. Recent DNA studies suggest that hummingbirds and swifts have a common ancestor and that both may belong in the order Caprimulgiformes that includes whip-poor-wills, nightjars, and nighthawks. Hummingbirds probably split from the swifts in the late Tertiary or perhaps in the late Cretaceous period (sixty-five to seventy mya), when a large plate broke loose from Gondwanaland to form South America. As a result of this later split from the swifts and the anatomical and behavioral differences between swifts and hummingbirds, some scientists suggest that hummingbirds should be in their own order.

The hummingbird family is the second largest family of birds in the Americas, with only the tyrant flycatchers, family Tyrannidae, having more species. The hummingbird family consists of more than 335 species and is divided into two subfamilies: Trochilinae, the typical hummingbirds or trochilids that includes most hummingbird species; and Phaethornithinae, the hermits, a small, relatively neutral-colored group. The number of species is not static. New species will almost certainly be discovered where research is ongoing in the remote forests along the Andes Mountain range in South America, and as scientists continue to study currently recognized groups, some species will be split into two or more species.

Question 6: What are the differences between typical or trochilid hummingbirds and hermits?

Answer: The typical hummingbird subfamily (Trochilinae) that has its center of diversification in the highlands of the Andes Mountains is much more diverse than the hermits (Phaethornithinae) that evolved in the lowlands of the Amazon River valley. A structural difference between the two families distinguishes them morphologically. All typicals or trochilids lack a tendon that attaches to a muscle from the humerus (upper wing bone) to stiffen the leading edge of the wing. Instead, the muscle attaches directly to the humerus. In the hermit group, a long tendon attaches the same muscle to the humerus.

Trochilid hummingbirds are diverse and colorful. Although in some species males and females look alike, most typical hummingbirds are sexually dimorphic, with males often having brilliant iridescent feathers and females usually lacking bright plumage. Their bills range in length from only 3/16 inch (5 millimeters) in the Purple-backed Thornbill (*Rhamphomicron microrhynchum*) to 4¾ inches (120 millimeters) in the Sword-billed Hummingbird (*Ensifera ensifera*), but they are characteristically not as curved as those of the hermit group. Males are almost always highly territorial, and the nests of trochilids are cup-shaped and usually suspended from a fork in a branch or built on top of a horizontal branch.

There are about thirty-four currently recognized species of hermits, as compared to about three hundred species of trochilids. Hermits are mostly neutral or dull in color, with plumage that is predominantly brown, gray, or reddish, without much iridescence except on the upper parts. Their habitat is in the dense scrub and tropical forest understory where there is little sunlight. All hermits have long bills that in most species are deeply curved for access to nectar in long tubular flowers. Both sexes are nonterritorial, and males gather in groups (leks) to display in order to attract females (see Chapter 4, Question 1: How does a hummingbird attract a mate?). Display behavior includes fanning the tail and opening the bill to reveal the brightly colored throat—orange, red, or yellow. Hermits' nests are conical, like long ice cream cones, and may be fastened to the side of a leaf of a large *Heliconia* plant or palm frond or hung from a vertical twig or other plant structure.

Question 7: How many species of hummingbirds are there in the world?

Answer: Scientists do not agree on the exact number of species because there has not been sufficient study of the DNA of all the species that are currently named and described to verify their uniqueness. The current lists consist of about 335 to 340 species, all living in North, Central, and South America. A new species of hummingbird, the Gorgeted Puffleg *Eriocnemis isabellaea*, was discovered as recently as 2007 in Colombia.

The hummingbird species most commonly seen in the United States are the Ruby-throated in the east and the Black-chinned in the west. Along the California coast and north to Alaska, Rufous and Anna's Hummingbird are the most common species. Fifteen species can be seen in summer in the sky islands—a region of 70,000 square miles that includes southeastern Arizona, southwestern New Mexico, and northwestern Mexico. The sky islands are mountain ranges in the desert that absorb rainfall and provide habitats for a diverse group of species that thrive in the range of climates that exist at different altitudes.

Question 8: How long do hummingbirds live?

Answer: The only way we know the life span of hummingbirds is to mark them in some way so that individuals can be identified from year to year, which is one reason why banding birds is so important. Each bird that is captured is given a uniquely numbered band that is recorded in a data base, and subsequent recapture allows us to find out how long the bird has lived since its first capture when it was banded (see Chapter 9, Question 5: Why do researchers band hummingbirds?).

William Calder, a distinguished University of Arizona ecology and evolutionary biology professor, recaptured hundreds of Broad-tailed Hummingbirds in Colorado. He was able to calculate that the average life span of this species was about two and one-half years, although that calculation is now considered low. Some now estimate that the average life span is between three and five years, and others give a range of six to twelve years. The recapture of hundreds of known-age birds by the Hummingbird Monitoring Network will help narrow this estimate in the next few years through its continuing studies related to the hummingbird population throughout the western states, southern Canada, and Mexico.

From 1984 through 2007, a total of 3,614 Ruby-throated Hummingbirds (*Archilochus colubris*) were banded at Hilton Pond Center for Piedmont Natural History near York, South Carolina. Constance Dustin Becker has been working in the Tumbesian region of southwestern Ecuador, collecting data for over ten years about the more than thirty hummingbird species that are native to the area. The analysis of all this data, including longevity information, needs to be peer reviewed and published so that interested scientists can make use of the information, and so that we can all learn more about how to conserve hummingbird populations.

The oldest wild hummingbird on record is a Broad-tailed Hummingbird that William Calder recaptured in Colorado that had been banded more than twelve years earlier. The Hummingbird Monitoring Network researchers have documented

Black-chinned Hummingbirds more than nine years old and Magnificent Hummingbirds more than eleven years old. While there is an organized banding program in Mexico run by the Instituto Manantlán de Ecologiá y Conservación de la Biodiversidad at the University of Guadalajara, there are no organized banding programs in Central and South America and we have no data for most of the hummingbird species that live in the tropical and subtropical Americas.

Few wild hummingbirds are banded as nestlings, but many are banded during their first summer of life, so their recapture tells us exactly how many years a bird has lived since it was hatched. There are a few hummingbird aviaries where juveniles are banded in the nest, and these birds can be followed annually until they die in captivity, although in captivity there is an uninterrupted supply of food and no threat of predation, so the typical lifespan of captives does not give a true picture of life in the wild.

Question 9: Which are the smallest and largest hummingbirds?

Answer: The smallest hummingbirds are the Reddish Hermit *Phaethornis ruber* from Guyana and Brazil and the Bee Hummingbird *Mellisuga helenae*, a resident of Cuba. These tiny individuals weigh less than a tenth of an ounce (1.6 to 1.9 grams), not even the weight of a penny (2.5 grams). Many of the woodstars, a group of hummingbirds in South America, also weigh less than 2 grams. In North America, the smallest hummingbird is the Calliope Hummingbird *Stellula calliope*, which breeds in the Rocky Mountains and is only slightly more than 2 inches long (about 6 centimeters) and weighs about 2.5 grams.

The Giant Hummingbird *Patagona gigas*, found in the Andes Mountains of South America, is the largest in the world, although at an adult weight of less than one ounce (26 grams) it is still a very small bird. From the tip of its bill to the end of its tail, one of these birds measures about 8½ inches (21 centimeters), almost twice as large as the next-largest hummingbird.

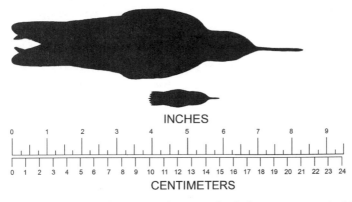

Figure 4. Comparison of the largest hummingbird, the Giant Hummingbird *Patagona gigas* from South America, and the smallest, the Bee Hummingbird *Mellisuga helanae* from the island of Cuba.

Jimmy McGuire, a specialist in phylogenetic analysis, suggests that this might mean the Giant Hummingbird has taken its own evolutionary path away from the other hummingbirds.

In North America, the largest hummingbirds are the Blue-throated *Lampornis clemenciae* and the Magnificent Hummingbird *Eugenes fulgens*, weighing on average about a quarter of an ounce (7 to 8 grams) and measuring about 5 inches long (12 centimeters), with slight variations due to sex and variations in the length of the bill.

The weight of a hummingbird changes throughout the day and in some species at different times of the year. Hummingbirds' weight is lowest in the early morning after a long night's sleep when their food has all been digested, the energy from the food has been burned, and the byproducts dissipated as water, carbon dioxide, and heat. Throughout the day, a bird will gain weight as it fills its crop with nectar and insects, and it will lose weight when it rests, resulting in an up-and-down pattern of body weight throughout the day. Within a twenty-four-hour period, the birds will be heaviest when they fill their crops in the evening to prepare for a long dark period when they cannot feed.

Most tropical hummingbirds do not make long-distance migratory flights, but hummingbirds that spend the summer in temperate latitudes become heaviest when they prepare for a migratory flight that can take several days or weeks to complete. These birds overeat and convert the sugars into fat that will provide energy during migration. In years when food is plentiful, some birds add so much fat that they double their normal body weight (see Chapter 5, "Flight and Migration").

There are several characteristics that help explain why even the largest hummingbird is so small. T. Ryan Gregory of the University of Guelph, Ontario, and colleagues found that hummingbirds have less DNA in their cells than is found in any other previously studied bird, reptile, or mammal. This supports the hypothesis that genome size is limited by the high metabolic demands of energy-intensive hovering in flight. They also have relatively smaller red blood cells and a smaller nucleus in each cell than is found in larger animals. Lighter bones and feathers and the highest heart and lung volume of any vertebrate contribute to the superior functioning of these miniature organisms.

TWO

Systems and Senses

Question 1: Are hummingbirds intelligent?

Answer: Hummingbirds are smart enough to have survived for millions of years, and if we take care of the earth, they will survive for millions more. Hummingbirds are well adapted to their environment. They know when to migrate, when to start nesting, and when it is time to return home. They know how to travel from their breeding ground to their wintering quarters and back. And since they are dependent on high energy sources at frequent intervals, they know where the flower patches are to get the sugar they need to survive all along their migration routes. They learn quickly and remember exactly where their food sources are located and when each resource will be available to them.

A bird lover in the eastern United States comments that "my hummingbird comes to my feeder location on the same day every spring. If the feeder is not there, he comes to the window and waits for me to hang it up." We notice that an experienced bird will look for the feeder in the exact position the feeder was in the last time he fed there. If you move the feeder left or right or up or down a few feet, the bird will first come to the feeder's original position and hover, looking for the feeding port. After a few seconds it will back off, explore, and find the new location. The bird will do this after being away in Mexico for six months. In our monitoring program, where we band hummingbirds throughout the spring, summer, and fall, we encounter the same birds from year to year, and we find that they return in spring within days of when we banded them the previous spring. Birds migrating south in the fall that stop at our monitoring stations arrive to replenish their energy supply within days of when we banded them or encountered them in the previous falls. We have followed this for up to nine years, and other banders have done the same.

We know that hummingbirds are a visual species, which means that they remember almost all their clues about the environment and other living things in visual terms. They remember enough detail about each habitat they encounter to decide whether to return or not, and if they return they know the exact location of whatever is of interest to them in relation to everything else in the area. They do not navigate by smell as do salmon, or by ultrasonic clicks like bats, but likely depend on sight to see the stars and the position of the sun for long-distance migration.

A hummingbird's fingertip-sized brain contains an amazing spatial atlas—something like Google Earth but in much greater detail. Their brain can accommodate all this visual information as well as the information necessary to keep them breathing, flying, hovering, reproducing, and surviving. One would hypothesize that the visual areas in the occipital lobe and the motor areas in the brain stem and elsewhere are particularly large. Enlarged motor areas could accommodate the complex motor skills a bird needs to simultaneously remain stable while hovering, its wings beating more than eighty times per second, and accurately insert the bill deeply into a flower—all on a windy day.

In 2006, Doug Wylie and Andrew Iwaniuk at the University of Alberta compared hummingbird brains with brains from twenty-eight other bird species. They hypothesized that hummingbird brains might be unique because of their wing speed and their ability to hover and fly forward and backward with great precision. The researchers found that the portion of the hummingbird brain that detects movement in the environment was proportionally two to five times larger than in any other species. This area is probably responsible, at least in part, for their exceptional optomotor response, which controls vision-related movement and allows them to see clearly enough to make precise feeding movements while hovering.

The passerine birds (songbirds like warblers, sparrows, wrens, thrushes, tanagers, finches, and jays) have the largest brains in relation to their body size. Hummingbirds' brains are relatively large in relation to body size but not as large as passerines'. In comparison, the brain of a chicken is small in relation to body size. The thinking about avian intelligence is summed up by neurobiologist Anton Reiner at the University of Tennessee: "While it was once thought that birds . . . were limited to instinctive behaviors, it is now clear that birds possess a well-developed cerebrum that . . . can support a cognitive ability that for some avian species rivals that in primates."

Question 2: What do hummingbirds eat?

Answer: The primary foods for hummingbirds are nectar and small arthropods like spiders and insects. Nectar from flowers provides sucrose as a source of energy, and insects provide protein and some fat to support growth and reproduction. If there are feeders available, birds normally drink from a feeder intermittently for two or more hours, beginning at sunrise, and then greatly reduce their dependency on nectar during the day, returning to the feeders an hour or so before sunset to fill up for the night. A hummingbird ingests about half its weight in sugar every day, and because most of its natural food is nectar that contains more than 75 percent water, hummingbirds rarely need to drink water. George West has observed hummingbirds drinking up to one-third of their body weight in a few minutes at a feeder. Apart from drinking nectar, they spend most of their feeding time hunting insects (see this chapter, Question 3: Why do hummingbirds need to eat so much?).

A popular area of research is hummingbirds' feeding preferences with regard to sugar composition (they prefer sucrose), concentration and viscosity of nectar, the fit of the bird's bill within the flower's corolla, and the color and position of the preferred flowers. Although hummingbirds frequently visit red tubular flowers, experiments have shown that the shape and color of the flower is less important than is its nectar supply. Hummingbirds quickly learn which plants provide the nectar they need, and they feed from those flowers on a regular basis. Various sources estimate that an average-sized hummingbird visits from one thousand to three thousand flowers every day. When feeding on flowers in the wild, the birds feed for only seconds at each flower because the nectar volume is so small, and they may move from flower to flower for as long as an hour until they obtain enough sugar. If hummingbirds are supplied with unlimited nectar at feeders, observations suggest that they need to drink nectar for only a few minutes every hour.

Plants provide nectar that contains multiple types of sugars, and a sample of seventeen species of flowers in Arizona and California showed that the amount of sucrose in their nectar ranged from 8 to 43 percent. Plants most preferred by hummingbirds have nectar that contains between 20 and 25 percent sucrose—sweeter than a typical cola drink—and they will not drink nectar with less than 12 percent sucrose. When Charles Blem of Virginia Commonwealth University and his colleagues offered Rufous Hummingbirds a choice of sucrose solutions ranging from 10 to 70 percent by increments of 10 percent, the birds most frequently chose the 50 percent solution. A high concentration of sugar allows the hummingbird to visit fewer flowers, but its digestive system limits how high a concentration it can quickly digest. Every time a hummingbird hovers in front of a flower, it uses food (energy) to gather food, so it must gather more than it expends.

To drink from a flower, a hummingbird inserts its long bill into a flower and laps up the nectar with its long, grooved tongue, much as a dog or cat laps water. The lick rate ranges from about five to thirteen licks per second depending on the size and anatomy of the bird, the volume of nectar in the flower, and the concentration of sugar in the nectar. Larger hummingbirds tend to have a slower lick rate than do smaller ones. Brian Collins of the Curtin University of Technology in Australia found that hummingbirds spend a longer time at flowers that have more nectar, because the high volume ingested per lick of the tongue makes the feeding process more energy efficient. When they feed from flowers with less nectar, the lick rate remains the same so the energy efficiency is reduced. When the nectar pool is small, only the tip of the tongue collects the solution and so the intake rate is considerably slower. When a flower's nectar is depleted, it is replaced in short order so that the nectar-feeding pollinators will continue to visit and fertilize the plants.

To gather the protein they need in their diet, hummingbirds forage for insects in various ways. The erratic movement made by the birds as they chase tiny insects and spiders is called gnatting. "Hawking" refers to catching insects while both the insect and the bird are in flight, and "gleaning" describes the hummingbird's hovering to snatch up insects that are sitting on the surfaces of leaves and branches. F. Gary Stiles, an American Museum of Natural History biologist working in Columbia, found that hermits apparently preferred gleaning spiders from their webs, while typicals employed all the usual methods. Insects also can play a more-than-supplementary role in the hummingbird diet, substituting for nectar when a dry spell causes a shortage of nectar-bearing flowers or when heavy rains make nectaring impossible. Insects are also the major protein source during a hummingbird's annual molt, and for females when they need protein and minerals to form eggs. Overwintering species in southeastern Arizona and in the eastern United States have to depend on insects and tree sap during the winter when no flowers are available. To access the sweet sap, they visit holes (sap wells) made in trees by woodpeckers and sapsuckers.

Pollination

In order for most plants to reproduce by producing seed or growing fruit they need to cross-fertilize, which means that male gametes (chromosome-carrying cells) from one plant must travel to another plant so they can fuse with its female gametes—this process is called pollination. The pollen of a few plants is transported in water (hydrophily), and in some species, the pollen is carried by the wind (anemophily), but about 80 percent of all plants are pollinated by living organisms that are usually drawn to the flowers for their nectar (biotic pollination). Pollinators include bees, butterflies, and other insects (entomophily), and vertebrates such as hummingbirds and bats (zoophily). There is some competition for nectar from the same flowers, but many species have preferences for flowers with certain shapes that provide them with fast, safe access, and they are selective about the sweetness, consistency, and composition of the nectar they seek. The result is that pollinators can usually share the resources of a habitat. The tubular-shaped flowers hummingbirds prefer hold nectar concentrated at their base. The male parts of

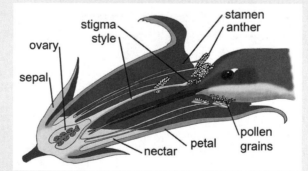

Cross-section of a tubular flower shows how the plant is formed to deposit pollen on the bird as it feeds and to pick up pollen carried on the bird's plumage at the same time.

Pollination

the flower are the stamens, with anthers at the ends that are covered with pollen grains that contain the male gametes. The female part of the flower is the pistil, made up of the stigma, style, and ovary. The ovary holds one or more ovules that contain the female gametes. The stigma is sticky so that pollen brushed against it will adhere to its surface. When this occurs, a pollen tube germinates from the pollen grains that have stuck to the stigma, and it grows down through the style into one of the ovules (seeds) in the ovary. Then the male gamete is released to fuse with the female gamete, and they form a fertilized seed that can develop into a new plant.

Hummingbirds are drawn to a flower by its shape and color, or because they know from experience that the flower contains the nectar that they need for food. When a hummingbird probes its bill into the flower to reach the nectar, pollen rubs off on the bill, head, or throat, depending on the species of flower and the location of its stamens. At the same time, the stigma of the pistil rubs against the bird, and pollen grains from a plant the bird visited earlier stick to the stigma. Since the bird may visit more than a thousand flowers a day, the chances are very good that it will transfer some pollen grains from one flower to the receptive female part of another flower of the same species, thus completing the act of pollination.

The great variety of hummingbird bills—from short and straight to very long and straight, and from short and curved to long and curved—developed as flowering plants developed in a process known as co-adaptation or coevolution. Natural selection caused both hummingbirds and plants to develop shapes that fit together, so that the bird depended on the flower for nectar and the flower depended on the bird for pollination. This beneficial association between bird and plant is called mutualism.

Question 3: Why do hummingbirds need to eat so much?

Answer: Since hummingbirds are the smallest of all warm-blooded animals, it may be difficult to understand why they need so much food each day. The reason has to do with the relationship between their body mass (weight) and their body surface from which heat is lost. Hummingbirds are homeotherms, which means they are animals that need to maintain a constant body temperature, independent of external conditions. Small birds have a small body mass, and they lose heat rapidly through their relatively large surface area, so they need more food per unit of body mass to stay normally warm. Large birds eat more and have more mass to produce heat, and they have proportionally less surface area from which heat is lost, so their thermal system is more efficient than the system of a smaller bird.

A 3.5-gram hummingbird requires about 7 kilocalories per day, or 2 kilocalories per gram of body weight, to maintain its normal body temperature. A larger bird like a sparrow, which weighs about 18 grams, requires about 15 kilocalories per day or 0.8 kilocalories per gram of body weight. A grouse that weighs about 600 grams requires more than 150 kilocalories per day, or 0.25 kilocalories per gram of body weight, and a human who weighs about 72,600 grams (160 pounds) requires 3,000 kilocalories per day, or 0.04 kilocalories per gram body weight. You can see that a hummingbird requires about fifty times more energy per gram of body weight than does a human.

These calculations are based on a constant ambient temperature of about 68 degrees Fahrenheit (20 degrees Celsius). As the ambient temperature falls, body-heat loss increases and so does the energy required to maintain a constant body temperature. Hummingbirds that live in cold climates at high elevations such as in the Andes Mountains, and species that migrate to the northern United States, Canada, and Alaska, can consume only so much food to make up for the heat lost at low temperatures. When they reach this limit, the birds must enter torpor to slow down their entire system or they die (see this chapter, Question 11: How do hummingbirds conserve energy?). The ambient temperature of a region therefore establishes a thermal boundary that limits the seasonal distribution of hummingbirds.

Question 4: How do hummingbirds know which flowers have nectar?

Answer: The flowers that produce nectar change daily, and hummingbirds must learn which flowers are rewarding every day so they do not waste time and energy exploring spent flowers.

Andrew Hurly from the University of Lethbridge, Alberta, and Susan Healy from Edinburgh University in Scotland found that Rufous Hummingbirds *Selasphorus rufus* were able to remember which flowers they had already visited, and they waited two to three hours before revisiting those flowers—the amount of time it took for the nectar to be replenished. The researchers were able to demonstrate that the birds remembered the exact location of the flowers during the entire summer season in Canada.

Hummingbirds use two nectar-foraging strategies: territoriality and traplining. Territoriality feeding is employed when either or both sexes of hummingbirds defend an area containing a flower patch against intruders. They spend most of their feeding time there, and when the flower patch declines in nectar production, they move to another patch and defend it. Traplining is used when resources are limited in the territory and the bird has to expand its search for food. In traplining, the bird feeds in a regular pattern, hovering at one flower and then the next in a patch, then going to another patch of flowers and moving through it flower by flower. This resembles the way a fur trapper would move through the woods checking his traps every day to see what he might have caught. A bird's foraging strategies can change based upon competition for and abundance of nectar plants. The relative number of trapliner versus territorial species is not well defined because some territorial species become trapliners given high competition and low nectar availability.

Frank Gill of the Academy of Natural Sciences studied the traplining behavior of Long-tailed Hermits *Phaethornis superciliosus,* now classified as Long-billed Hermits *Phaethornis longirostris,* by color marking individuals. He found that they adjusted to nectar availability (the rate at which nectar was replenished), but if there was competition for nectar, they visited the sources more frequently.

Rebecca Irwin at the University of Vermont tried to learn how hummingbirds know which flowers have the most nectar. She manipulated variables such as flowers with holes made by nectar-robbing bees (which suggest that the nectar supply has been depleted), visual cues (she moved plants around so that spatial memory was not a factor); and translucency, which might reveal the presence of nectar (she painted the corollas of the flowers to eliminate any visual cues). In all her experiments, she found that the hummingbirds still visited significantly more plants with nectar, somehow able to determine its presence. Other researchers have confirmed these findings (see also this chapter, Question 13: Do hummingbirds have a good sense of smell?).

Question 5: How do hummingbirds digest their food?

Answer: Hummingbirds are constantly digesting food and refueling their bodies, and estimates of how fast nectar is digested and passes through their system range from only a few minutes to as much as an hour. Scientists agree that hummingbirds convert to usable fuel almost 100 percent of the sugars in the nectar they consume, perhaps the highest use-ratio of any food by any animal. Although the birds digest and excrete most food within thirty minutes, insect and spider remains have been documented to pass through a White-eared Hummingbird *Hylocharis leucotis* in less than ten minutes. Any water that the hummingbird absorbs from its food that is not used for hydration is extracted by the kidneys and excreted.

A hummingbird's tongue is forked at the tip and each fork has a number of grooves into which the nectar is trapped through capillary action. When the bird retracts the tongue into its mouth, the nectar is in essence squeezed out of the tongue and swallowed. Nectar and solid food (insect material) pass down the esophagus and land in the crop, a small thin-walled pouch in which the solid food is moistened with mucous. The nectar continues on, bypassing the stomach and reaching the small intestine, where the sugar is absorbed. Once the crop is full, it takes about four minutes for it to empty of nectar and only fifteen minutes for all the sugar in the nectar to be absorbed in the intestine.

The sugar from nectar is mostly in the form of sucrose. During times of high energy demand when the bird is feeding and flying, the liver converts the sugar to glucose, a more simple carbohydrate that is burned (metabolized) more quickly by the body. When intake of sugar exceeds the need for its immediate metabolism, the liver converts the sugar to fat that is stored for use overnight or for migratory flight. Digestion of solid food begins in the proventriculus, part of the bird's stomach. Here, hydrochloric acid and the enzyme pepsin begin the breakdown of the insects and other solids. The food is passed along to the gizzard or ventriculus, the second part of the stomach, where

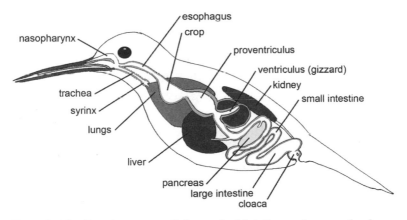

Figure 5. The digestive system of a hummingbird. Organ placement has been altered for visibility in this diagram. Normally, the intestines are longer and folded over each other, concealing the organs.

two large muscles rub together to grind it up. Most birds eat grit, stones, or sand that mix with the food and act as teeth in the stomach, helping to chew or break down the food. Since hummingbirds eat only small insects, the hummingbird gizzard is not well developed. Hummingbirds have been seen consuming fine sand that could be a source of grit for the grinding of insect parts in the gizzard, as is commonly seen in other birds, but they may also eat sand to obtain minerals like calcium. Food is further digested by liver bile and pancreatic enzymes in the small intestine, and indigestible materials are passed into the large intestine where water is absorbed. The solid remains collect in the cloaca, where they are mixed with urine from the kidneys and excreted.

Question 6: How do hummingbirds get rid of the water from all that nectar they drink?

Answer: Because they feed on liquid nectars, hummingbirds have an extremely high rate of water turnover, up to two or more times their body weight each day. The water along with the sugar in the nectar is absorbed in the intestine, and all the water not needed for normal body hydration is transported in the blood to the kidneys. Hummingbirds' kidneys and intestinal tract do not absorb water as readily as do those of other animals, helping to avoid water intoxication, a potentially fatal brain dysfunction from drinking too much water. The result is that hummingbirds produce urine, unlike most birds, which instead excrete semi-solid uric acid.

Physiological ecologist Carlos Martinez del Rio along with Bradley Hartman Bakken and colleagues at the University of Wyoming examined the function of the kidneys of Broad-tailed Hummingbirds *Selasphorus platycercus* and Green-backed Firecrowns *Sephanoides sephanoides* to try to understand how they balance the need to eliminate large quantities of water with their susceptibility to dehydration when they are not feeding. They found that the birds' kidneys were very sensitive to the lack of water, and that the rate of excretion slowed down or stopped when water was in short supply, minimizing the risk of dehydration. The poorly developed kidneys in hummingbirds do not have as many nephrons (filters that extract salts and waste products from the blood) as are found in mammalian kidneys and those of other birds.

In the hummingbird, excess water that was absorbed in the intestine passes into the bloodstream, and along with salts and waste products it is removed by the kidneys. This fluid (urine) drains from the kidneys through tubes (ureters) into the cloaca, a baglike structure at the end of the large intestine (see figure 5), and it is expelled as it is produced. When a hummingbird gets ready to take off, a stream of urine squirts out of the cloaca, lightening the bird's weight and so making flight easier. The cloacal muscles propel the urine and feces away from the bird, which helps keep the animal clean and also keeps the waste products away from the bird's perching area and nest so the odor doesn't attract predators. Even nestling hummingbirds participate in keeping their area clean, instinctively turning their rear ends toward the rim of the nest and squirting their urine and waste up and over the edge.

Question 7: Why do hummingbirds have such long bills?

Answer: The only flowers that attract hummingbirds are those that collect sucrose-rich nectar in a receptacle from which a hummingbird can drink. Flat flowers like dandelions and asters may produce some nectar, but it does not collect in significant quantity. Other flowers produce nectar that is high in glucose or fructose, sugars that hummingbirds cannot easily digest. Tubular flowers have relatively long corollas (petals that are fused together to make a tube), creating a cup where a large volume of nectar can collect. To get at the nectar, a pollinator must have either a very long bill or a long tongue. Some flowers pollinated by hummingbirds have short corollas that contain nectar, and hummingbirds that drink nectar from them usually have shorter bills. Some flowers have evolved along with their pollinators so that only a specific group of pollinators can feed from that flower (see Co-adaptation sidebar in Chapter 1), and other flowers invite competition from bats, other insectivorous birds, bees, and butterflies.

Many nectar-rich flowers dangle at the end of very thin stems, so a bird must be able to hover in front of the flower in order to

Other Nectar Drinkers

Many animals drink nectar from flowers. Those that we often see during the day include ants, butterflies, bees, and other insects, but others are not obvious. At night, several species of nectar-feeding bats push their noses into flowers and with their long tongues lap up as much nectar as they can while briefly hovering in front of the flower, dropping away and returning many times to drain the nectar from a single blossom. In the process, the bat's fur is dusted with pollen that it transfers to another plant. Barbara French and Carol Butler describe how nectar-feeding bats are important pollinators for many species of desert flowers and are strong competitors with hummingbirds for nectar. The hundreds of plant species that depend on bats for pollination include mangos, bananas, guavas, plantains, avocados, dates, peaches, and breadfruit.

In southern Mexico and in central and northern South America a group of birds called Flowerpiercers (genus *Diglossa*) take nectar from flowers without providing pollination. To steal the nectar, Flowerpiercers tear a hole in the base of a flower with the sharp hook on the tip of their bill—some bees and wasps steal nectar this way too, either making a hole themselves or taking advantage of a hole already present. Other birds in more northern climates that steal nectar clip or tear off the petals of the flower and then dip into the remaining cup to sip up the nectar. All these birds compete with hummingbirds for a valuable resource.

Figure 6. The dustlike substance on the head of this male Anna's Hummingbird *Calypte anna is* yellow pollen from the anthers of flowers the bird recently visited.

probe it and extract its nectar, something at which hummingbirds are expert. While other species of birds have long bills—sandpipers and herons, for example—no other bird can hover in front of a flower and probe into the well of nectar at its base to extract the sugar solution.

Question 8: How can hummingbirds be so active?

Answer: Hummingbirds have a constant need for oxygen to power their active lives. The larger hummingbirds take in around 180 breaths per minute, and small hummingbirds at rest about 275 breaths per minute. By comparison, humans at rest breathe about sixteen times per minute. When a hummingbird flies with its wings moving from twenty to two hundred beats per second, its respiration rate rises to as many as five hundred breaths per minute, because the contraction of the wing muscles powers its respiratory system. The intake of air at that rate of speed provides ample oxygen to convert glucose into energy in a hummingbird's flight muscles.

Scientists are interested in understanding the nuances and limits of hummingbirds' energy exchange. In research conducted by Kenneth Welch and Raul Suarez at the University of California, Santa Barbara, along with Douglas Altshuler of the University of California, Riverside, Anna's and Rufous Hummingbirds, after fasting during the night, were released into a cage with feeders fitted with respiratory masks. By analyzing the air drawn through the mask, the researchers established that the birds rapidly (in twenty to thirty minutes) shifted from metabolizing stored fat to burning the carbohydrates in the sugar solution they were drinking. Using mathematical models to calculate the rate of oxygen consumption, they concluded that hummingbirds are "carbohydrate maximizers," as Welch put it. If nectar is available, hummingbirds use it for fuel instead of tapping into their fat reserves. This has implications for their ability to hover at high altitudes where oxygen is scarce, refueling directly from the nectar as they drink it instead of depleting their fat reserves.

Douglas Altshuler along with Robert Dudley and Jimmy McGuire of the University of California, Berkeley, studied the effect on hummingbirds of the lower levels of oxygen available at the high altitudes where hummingbirds are common. They studied the flight performance of forty-three Andean species and found that their ability to hover in the thin air was facilitated by having larger wings and by making a wider sweep of their wings (larger stroke amplitude), compared to hummingbirds hovering at lower altitudes. They also measured the birds' strength (power) at high elevations by attaching a string of beads to the body of each bird and filming the bird as it tried to lift off the floor of the cage. By adding beads, they could determine the limits of the birds' power. They reported that birds at high altitude had less power for activities like ascending and chasing, two modes of flight that are important in hummingbirds. This loss of maneuverability would affect birds' ability to avoid or repel predators and to assert control over their territory. The researchers conclude that this increased energetic cost of living at high elevations may be the reason more hummingbirds do not take advantage of the abundance of flowers and the dearth of bird and insect predators high in the mountains.

Christopher Witt of the University of New Mexico along with Dudley, McGuire, and other colleagues, explored this issue of oxygen consumption with hummingbirds in a flight chamber in which the oxygen concentration was manipulated by the researchers. Their goal was to see at what point there was simply not enough oxygen for the birds to be able to hover. They found that even lowland species were able to hover at oxygen levels equivalent to the peak of Mt. Everest, although birds that were adapted to the lowest elevations (sea level to 4,600 feet or 1,400 meters) had a more difficult time.

Birds have a unique system to transfer oxygen from the air into the bloodstream and the carbon dioxide waste product from the blood back into the air. Not having a diaphragm like mammals, they draw in air by the movement of their body musculature. When birds fly, their flight muscles pump air in and out of their respiratory system, exchanging the air through the nostrils (nares). The hummingbird's nares are not easy to see, as a protective flap of keratinous tissue covers the openings. Air flows through the nasopharynx (nose-to-throat cavity) and down into the trachea (windpipe), just as in mammals. Instead of a larynx (the voice box in mammals), birds have a syrinx lower in the trachea.

Some of the incoming air bypasses the lungs through tiny passages called parabronchi and enters thin membranous air sacs that occupy spaces between the organs and inside the larger hollow bones. The rest of the air enters the lungs through the two bronchi, where there are very fine air tubules lined with capillaries in which the exchange of gases to and from the blood takes place. The air that was diverted into the air sacs upon inspiration is pumped back out through the lungs upon expiration (breathing out). This system allows fresh, oxygen-rich air to flow through the lungs on both inspiration and expiration, doubling the efficiency of the gas exchange.

Question 9: Are hummingbirds warm blooded or cold blooded?

Answer: Hummingbirds are, like humans, warm-blooded creatures, or homeotherms, maintaining a relatively high and constant body temperature that varies according to time of day. Their average daytime body temperature is higher than that of humans, about 104 to 108 degrees Fahrenheit, or 40 to 42 degrees Celsius. Their body temperature is highest when they are active during the day, especially when they are flying and hovering, and lowest at night when they are sleeping. On warm nights, they maintain their temperature at around thirty-nine degrees Celsius, but on cold nights, their body temperature can drop to as low as eighteen degrees Celsius, just high enough to maintain normal body function but low enough to conserve energy. This energy-saving state is called hypothermia or torpor, and without being able to slow down their metabolism in this way, they could run out of energy and die (see this chapter, Question 11: How do hummingbirds conserve energy?).

Hummingbirds have fewer feathers than do any other birds, and therefore the insulation they gain from feathers is poor. Birds with more feathers and more dense feathers can fluff them to increase the insulating layer against the cold. Because hummingbirds are limited in this ability, they have to rely on metabolic heat to maintain their body temperature. Metabolic heat is derived from the metabolism or breakdown of foods (primarily glucose) in the muscles as they contract. The metabolism of glucose and other basic foods releases water, carbon dioxide, and heat as the major byproducts. The water is filtered by the kidneys and voided as urine, the carbon dioxide is conveyed to the lungs by the bloodstream and exhaled by respiration, and the heat keeps the bird warm but is also radiated to the surrounding air and lost.

Question 10: How fast does a hummingbird's heart beat?

Answer: Relative to body weight, hummingbirds have the largest hearts of all birds. A hummingbird's heart represents about 2 percent of its weight. Their metabolism is higher than that of larger birds because they lose heat faster. In order to keep energy and oxygen supplied to their tissues, hummingbirds must have a strong heart capable of a very fast contraction rate or heartbeat. At rest, a hummingbird's heart may beat as few as five hundred times per minute, but normally it beats nearer to one thousand times per minute. When the bird is highly active, the rate can rise to twelve hundred beats per minute, and when a hummingbird enters torpor, its heart rate may slow to as few as about fifty beats per minute (see this chapter, Question 11: How do hummingbirds conserve energy?).

For the same reason that their heart rate is so fast, hummingbirds' respiration or breathing rate must also be very fast to keep the oxygen supplied to the tissues and to remove the carbon dioxide from the body. Co-author West measured breathing rates of small hummingbirds at rest at about 275 breaths per minute. When the birds are active, this rate may rise to more than 500 breaths per minute. In comparison, larger birds like pigeons or sparrows generally breathe only about 30 times per minute.

Question 11: How do hummingbirds conserve energy?

Answer: Hummingbirds conserve energy by slowing down their metabolism, heartbeat, and respiration rate, and entering a state of hypothermia or torpor. This is different than sleep, when the heart and respiration rates slow only slightly and the temperature may fall just a few degrees. Arousal from sleep can be almost instantaneous. When a bird is in torpor, the decrease in the rates of body function and the drop in body temperature are significantly greater and it takes several minutes to as long as an hour for a bird to warm up and become fully functional. Hummingbirds enter torpor at night when the ambient temperature drops below a comfortable level, or when their energy reserves are low. They can remain in this state for as long as fourteen hours.

Hummingbirds rest with their feathers fluffed to maximize their insulating ability, their body covering their feet to minimize heat loss and their bill pointed upward at an angle. They do not bury their head under their wing, as do many songbirds. Arousing from this state can take up to an hour for larger species, and their body temperature must reach about 102 degrees Fahrenheit (39 degrees Celsius) before they can fly. Like all birds and mammals, they have a circadian rhythm or biological clock that tells them when to wake in the morning and start to raise their body temperature back to normal. They do this by shivering—rapid contraction of the skeletal musculature (mostly the pectoral or flight muscles)—which produces heat and raises their internal temperature.

Many animals use similar strategies to conserve energy when conditions require it. For example, some bats enter a state of torpor for several days at a time when temperatures drop, and other mammals and birds either enter torpor or slow down even

Figure 7. Costa's Hummingbird *Calypte costae* in torpor at night, its eyes closed and feathers fluffed for warmth.

more and hibernate when it is very cold. When it is very hot and dry, the same protective state is called estivation, and some desert butterflies estivate in the pupal stage until rain stimulates plant growth so that nectar is available when they emerge.

Question 12: Can hummingbirds walk?

Answer: Hummingbirds can shift from side to side on a perch by shuffling one foot after the other, and they can stand on one foot for hours if they need to, but they do not walk step by step in a forward direction. Hummingbirds are so reliant on their flying ability they never bother to move their feet except to scratch, move eggs in the nest, or lash out at an opponent. In order to change position on the perch, they fly up, hover, and settle back down. They do use their legs and feet as radiators—that is, to radiate heat into the air when they get too hot from constant hovering. In hot weather you will notice the feet hanging down while the bird hovers at a flower or feeder, but in cold weather the feet are pulled up into the belly feathers to conserve heat.

Question 13: Do hummingbirds have a good sense of smell?

Answer: The importance of the sense of smell in birds is not well understood. Many hummingbird-pollinated flowers have relatively little fragrance, which may contribute to the assumption that the perception of odors is not an important factor in the birds' ability to find food. They have excellent vision, and most research concludes that they rely primarily on visual and auditory stimuli. While that may be correct, the importance of their ability to detect odors appears to have been undervalued.

One measure of a bird's ability to detect odors is the ratio of the size of the olfactory bulb to the size of the brain. The relative size of the olfactory bulb in five species of hummingbirds studied by Paolo Ioale and Floriano Papi varies about thirteenfold. These anatomical investigations were part of research they conducted in Brazil in which they studied White-vented Violet-ear

Colibri serrirostris hummingbirds in captivity, and were able to train them to successfully discriminate among several smells in the laboratory, including lavender, jasmine, eucalyptus, amyl acetate, turpentine, and no odor.

Yale biologists Kenneth Goldsmith and Timothy Goldsmith observed Black-chinned Hummingbirds *Archilochus alexandri* in the wild to test their ability to use odors to find food. Birds were trained to associate the odor of ethyl butyrate (it has a smell like Juicy Fruit chewing gum) with a feeder containing a 30 percent sucrose solution. A small vial containing the fragrance and a wick to disperse it were attached to the feeders to create this association. Then two additional feeders were installed in the area, each containing a 2 to 3 percent saline solution (not an attractive food source for the birds). During the experiments, the positions of the four feeders were rotated so the birds could not associate a particular location with a food source, and the fragrance-filled vials were rotated among the feeders. The birds were observed to initially approach a feeder that had the ethyl butyrate odor 60 percent of the time, indicating that the odor played more than a chance role in their choice. Running the same tests with slight color differences among the solutions, the birds were able to choose the right feeder with far greater accuracy and three times as quickly, confirming the primacy of their ability to use visual cues.

Some plants that have repellent odors take time during flowering to produce flowers with an attractive smell for pollinators. Kessler and colleagues at the Max Planck Institute of Chemical Ecology in Germany found that common tobacco plants produce benzyl acetone along with nicotine in the nectar that entices Black-chinned Hummingbirds to pollinate the flowers. While this may be good for the tobacco plant, the effect of the nicotine intake on the hummingbirds is unknown.

Recent analysis of the nine bird genomes that had been completed by the date of the publication of this book (none of the birds were hummingbirds) suggests that the sense of smell in birds may have more importance than had been formerly believed, according to Silke Steiger and her colleagues at the

Max Planck Institute for Ornithology in Germany and at the Cawthron Institute in New Zealand. For example, the sense of smell is highly developed in vultures and other carrion eaters. It is clear we do not have the final word on the importance for birds of the sense of smell, but research in this area is moving forward.

Question 14: Do hummingbirds hear well?

Answer: All birds have a well-developed sense of hearing, but because the cochlea of the inner ear is shorter in birds, their frequency range is probably more limited than in mammals. The structure of a bird's ear is similar to the mammalian ear, but the outer ear does not have the large external component, or pinna, you see in dogs or humans. Instead, a bird's outer ear is a short tube with an opening to the outside that is usually hidden beneath feathers on the side of the head. You can see the external ear by gently lifting feathers on the side of the head behind the eyes. In birds with no feathers on the head, as in many species of vultures, the opening is apparent. Although the decorative feathers on top of the Great Horned Owl's head appear to be ears or horns, that bird too has external ear openings on the sides of its head.

The short tube of the outer ear ends inside the head at the eardrum (tympanum), which divides the outer from the middle ear. In mammals, three tiny bones (ossicles) transmit the sound waves that reach the tympanum to the inner ear, but birds have only one ear ossicle, the columella. The columella in the middle ear transmits sound vibrations from an air medium to a liquid medium in the inner ear. The sound waves in fluid then enter the cochlea, where the sensory hair cells are located. When these are stimulated, they transmit the information to the brain via the auditory nerve and the brain interprets the signals as sound. Bernard Lohr and Robert Dooling found that tests using electrodes on a hummingbird's auditory nerve indicated that a Ruby-throated Hummingbird hears best at frequencies ranging from about 2,000 to 3,000 hertz (cycles per second); sensitivity declined rapidly below and above this range. In comparison, a normal adult human can hear sound from around 500 to 20,000 hertz.

Carolyn Pytte, Millicent Ficken, and Andrew Moiseff recorded singing from a Blue-throated Hummingbird that ranged far into the ultrasonic frequency at 30,000 hertz. Sounds were routinely produced at frequencies of 20,000 hertz, but when the birds were tested in the laboratory, they could not hear anything

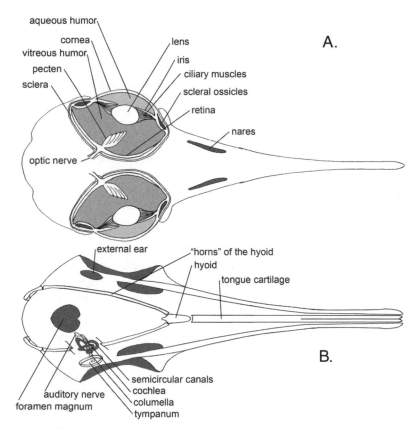

Figure 8. The skull of a hummingbird: *A*, view from the top showing the features of the eyes. Note how large the eyes are and how much space they occupy in the skull; *B*, view from below showing the details of the ear and the tongue apparatus (hyoid). The spinal cord exits the brain through the foramen magnum.

above 7,000 hertz. This leaves us to wonder why the birds are producing sounds that they cannot hear.

Question 15: Do hummingbirds have good eyesight?

Answer: Hummingbirds have excellent eyesight, significantly better than that of humans. Even though their eyes are relatively tiny, they are proportionally large for the size of the bird. Human eyes are globular or almost spherical in shape, as are most mammalian eyes, but birds' eyes are flatter on the front surface and only the cornea protrudes outward (see figure 8). To conserve weight, the muscles that move the eye are greatly reduced in most birds and the eyes are more fixed in position in the skull. Most of the time, hummingbirds have to move their whole head in order to see in different directions. They can move their eyes in their sockets to a limited degree, as revealed in a slow-motion video sequence of a feeding Purple-throated Mountain-gem *Lampornis calolaema* taken by videographer Thomas Kaminski (personal communication). The bird's pupil can be seen shifting from looking forward to looking backward as it feeds, but this kind of eye motion has rarely been documented.

The hummingbird eye is constructed much as a mammalian eye, with a cornea, iris, sclera, lens, anterior chamber with aqueous humor (watery fluid), posterior chamber with vitreous humor (gel-like fluid), and a retina. In mammals, the retina is maintained by a network of blood capillaries over its inside surface. In a bird's eyes, a comblike structure, the pecten, protrudes into the posterior chamber. It is loaded with blood vessels and nourishes the retina via the vitreous humor.

Like other birds that are active during the day, hummingbirds have a preponderance of retinal cone cells that distinguish colors. The retina's rods distinguish only light and dark, so vision with rods is like looking at a black and white photograph in shades of gray. Some species of hummingbirds have excellent night vision and have been seen feeding after sunset and before sunrise. The hummingbird eye is focused, as it is in mammals, by contracting the shape of the lens with muscles that are attached around the rim. Some species of hawks can see greater detail at a distance than humans can—their resolution ability is about two and one-half times better—but most birds have about the same visual acuity as humans. We do not know if humming-birds have especially acute vision, but there is no doubt that they can see very well, as they can spot a rival from a long distance and move rapidly to chase it away.

Because the hummingbird's eyes are on the sides of the head, the birds do not have good binocular vision, which judges depth of field. Many birds bob their heads to estimate how far away a subject is in relation to other things that they can see. This rapid movement gives them views of the object from two differ-ent angles, and in that way they obtain the information needed to judge its distance. The advantage of having eyes on the sides of its head is that a hummingbird can see in front and almost all the way around behind itself. If you watch a perched humming-bird, you will see its head continuously move slightly left and right as it gets a 360-degree view of its surroundings. In this way, it stays alert for potential predators, rivals, territorial invaders, and mates.

We know that hummingbirds have good color vision, and it is suspected that they can also see into the ultraviolet part of the spectrum. Timothy Goldsmith, a biologist from Yale University, found that three species of hummingbirds retain oil droplets in the cone cells of the retina that allow them to see some ul-traviolet light. This may help them recognize flowers with ultra-violet nectar guides, also used by bees and butterflies to locate the nectar source within a flower. The ability to see ultraviolet light is helpful in navigation on cloudy days when the sun is ob-scured, because the ultraviolet rays from the sun penetrate the cloud layer (see Chapter 5, Question 4: How do hummingbirds find their way during migration?). The sun generates patterns of polarized light, especially in the ultraviolet range, and these patterns indicate the location of the sun when it is not directly visible. Polarized ultraviolet receptors in the bird's eye are con-figured in such a way that they can derive directional informa-tion from polarized light.

Question 16: Do hummingbirds hum?

Answer: Although hummingbirds have a voice box called a syrinx, their ability to hum is not produced vocally but through rapid wing movement. The larger hummingbirds, who beat their wings around twenty times per second, produce a sound like a tiny helicopter—your ears can almost distinguish the individual beats (see Chapter 3, Question 1: How fast does a hummingbird beat its wings?). Smaller hummingbirds beat their wings around eighty times per second or even faster, and this produces a more continuous hum as the air is compressed by the wings on both the up and down stroke. Some hummingbirds have stiff tail feathers that vibrate when the bird flies rapidly, and this may create humming or other sounds that are used in courtship and territory defense (see Chapter 4, Question 1: How does a hummingbird attract a mate?).

Christopher Clark took high-speed video of a male Anna's Hummingbird during its courtship dives and found that it produces a loud chirp by spreading its tail feathers for sixty milliseconds, faster than you can blink your eye. He experimented with male Red-billed Streamertail Hummingbirds *Trochilus polytmus*, which have elongated tail streamers. These tail feathers had been credited with producing their distinctive whirring flight sound, but he found that tailless Streamertails could still produce the sound in his flight cages. By manipulating the wing feathers, he established that the sound is produced by a slight displacement in flight of two wing feathers (primary eight and nine).

Other hummingbirds also have modified primary wing feathers that produce a sound. The adult male Broad-tailed Hummingbird *Selasphorus platycercus* can produce a trilling sound as it flies because of modifications in the ninth and tenth primary feather tips. The tenth or outermost primary is almost needle-shaped at the tip and the ninth is cut off at the tip. Females and juveniles do not have their feathers modified in this way, so only the adult males can produce the sound, which may be used in courtship and in warning other birds away from their feeding area. Todd Hunter studied the effect of wing sounds of male

Calliope and Rufous Hummingbirds on males and females of the same species and of other species. He found that the wing sound or trill of the male wings during normal flight altered the behavior of both sexes, but more that of females. He believes that wing sounds are one important method of communication among hummingbirds.

The humming sound differs with wing-beat frequency to such a degree that a trained ear can distinguish certain species in the garden by the pitch of the hum. Perhaps early biologists who first encountered hummingbirds in the Americas heard them long before they saw them and asked, "What are those hum-

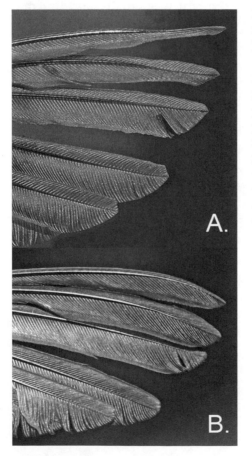

Figure 9. Wing tips of adult male (*A*) and female (*B*) Broad-tailed Hummingbirds *Selasphorus platycercus*, showing the differences in the outer two feathers, primary ten at the top, and primary nine below it. The female has conventional feathers, but the male's outer two primaries are modified to allow him the option of creating a loud trilling sound when he flies.

ming birds?" Birds are sometimes named for their call or song (chickadee, kiskadee, towhee); hummingbirds are probably the only ones named for the sound produced by their wings. The Bumblebee Hummingbird *Atthis heloisa* of central and southern Mexico was so named not because it resembles bumblebee, but because its wing hum sounds like that of a bumblebee. While the word "hummingbird" is part of the species name for many birds, it is used as a common name (originally "humming birds") only in the United States and Canada—it is not translated to describe the bird in other languages. Other countries and languages have their own names for these birds, such as *zunzu'n* in Cuba, mimicking their sound; *oiseau-mouche* (fly-sized bird) in French; and *beija flor* (kiss the flower) in Portuguese. Spanish has several variations: in Mexico the common names are *colibri* and *chupaflor* (sip or suck the flower), and in Chile it is *pica flor* (peck the flower).

Question 17: Do hummingbirds sing?

Answer: Hummingbirds are one of few bird families that learn their song from other birds of the same species shortly after fledging. Only the oscines (songbirds), members of the order Passeriformes (perching birds), parrots, and hummingbirds apparently learn their songs instead of inheriting the vocal pattern from their parents. Hummingbirds are quite noisy, but most of their harsh and unmelodic vocalizations are considered calls rather than songs. They make sounds typically described as squeaks, rasps, chirps, or buzz trills. When they are foraging for nectar from one flower to the next, a bird often produces what is called a chip note, alerting other birds to its presence. Different species make different sounds in this situation, and you can guess which species is at your feeder by listening to the sounds. When a hummingbird is disturbed, it may make a series of these sounds.

Colorful hummingbirds use their iridescent colors in breeding displays, where another bird would use song. They also use visual displays to chase intruders from their territory, and generally use more physical than vocal aggression when trying to communicate. Hermits, the drab-colored tropical humming-birds, vocalize more than do their colorful counterparts. The males gather in leks (groups) and vocalize to attract females (see Chapter 4, Question 1: How does a hummingbird attract a mate?).

Some tropical hummingbirds have songs that last thirty seconds or more and are more complex than those of their North American counterparts, according to Josep del Hoyo. Some typical colorful male hummingbirds sing like songbirds while perched at the edge of their feeding or courting territory. Millicent Ficken of the University of Wisconsin-Milwaukee and others studied the combative vocalizations of different species of hummingbirds. They found that Black-chinned Hummingbirds display a complex variety of vocal sounds, and Blue-throated Hummingbirds sing a "whisper song" in the riparian forests of the desert sky islands in southeastern Arizona that ranges from 2,000 to 8,000 hertz and lasts about two and one-half seconds. Blue-throated females have a shorter and less varied song than that of the male. Ficken and colleagues conducted experiments in which they broadcast creek noises at various sound levels while the birds they were studying were making sounds, and they found that males of this species modified their sounds in response to changes in the level of ambient noise. At times, their songs contained ultrasonic frequencies beyond the range of their own hearing (the researchers measured brainstem responses to determine what the birds could hear). The purpose of these sounds is unknown, but clearly they are not for intraspecies communication, since they are not audible.

Anna's Hummingbird has a song that runs for about seven seconds with a series of different notes, all in the 8,000-hertz range. (To give you an idea of how 8,000 hertz sounds, the highest note on an eighty-eight-key piano is 4,186 hertz.) Bethany Williams and Anne Houtman at California State University recently found that Costa's Hummingbird of the southern California deserts sings a shorter song of four notes that lasts about two and one-half seconds in the range of 6,000 to 11,000 hertz.

Magnificent Hummingbirds sing a whisper song in the 8,000-hertz range on their territory. These species also have many call or chip notes, some of which are probably used in different situations. Some hummingbirds can imitate or mimic the sounds of other hummingbirds, a skill they use to gain access to a neighbor's feeding territory.

THREE

Feathers and Bones

Question 1: How fast does a hummingbird beat its wings?

Answer: To the human eye, anything over twelve wing beats per second appears simply as a blur, and hummingbird wing beats are definitely in the blur category. When the male Ruby-throated Hummingbird is courting, its wing speed may accelerate up to two hundred beats per second during its aerial display. Although the rapid display occurs only briefly, this is said to be the fastest wing beat of any bird (see also Chapter 4, Question 1: How does a hummingbird attract a mate?). A mosquito, by contrast, although it is feather-light, must beat its tiny wings about one thousand times each second in order to stay in the air. In comparison, a big butterfly with a large wing surface area may beat its wings as slowly as four times per second.

Average-sized Ruby-throated *Archilochus colubris* and Rufous Hummingbirds *Selasphorus rufus* beat their wings approximately forty to fifty times each second. Wing-beat rates range from about eight to ten beats per second for the largest species, the Giant Hummingbird *Patagona gigas,* and up to eighty beats per second for a tiny Amethyst Woodstar *Calliphlox amethystina.* The larger hummingbirds in the United States, the Magnificent *Eugenes fulgens* and the Blue-throated *Lampornis clemenciae,* average about twenty-two wing beats per second.

Why do hummingbirds have to beat their wings so fast? Because the extent of their wing surface area is relatively small

compared to their body weight. Imagine an eagle or a hawk flying overhead, and note that the surface of its wings is very large
compared with the size of its body. These birds can even glide
and soar *without* beating their wings. It is impossible to imagine
a hummingbird gliding. They have to beat their relatively small
wings constantly just to stay airborne, although while they are
airborne they have unique mobility (see this chapter, Question 2:
How does a hummingbird hover?).

With all this beating of the wings, are hummingbirds fast flyers? There is a limited amount of data measuring the speed of
their flight, and more comparative research would be useful.
Christopher Clark of the University of California, Berkeley, ex-
perimentally lengthened (by adding long feathers), shortened,
and removed the tails of different Anna's Hummingbirds and
then measured their speed and the metabolic cost of flight in
a wind tunnel. He concluded that longer, shorter, and removed
tails all slowed down the birds, and that they flew fastest when
their tails were of normal length. An elongated tail was metabolically most costly, increasing the cost of flight up to 11 percent.
But we don't know whether a naturally long-tailed hummingbird flies slower and at a higher metabolic cost than the same
body-weight hummingbird with a shorter tail.

A Ruby-throated Hummingbird has been timed by William
Calder and Lorene Calder of the University of Arizona flying
at 24 miles per hour, and Stephen Russell, a hummingbird biologist also from the University of Arizona, recorded Anna's
Hummingbirds in the wild flying up to 45 miles per hour during brief dive displays (he measured their normal speed in sustained linear flight at just over 17 miles per hour). James Clark of
the University of California, Berkeley, filmed Anna's Hummingbirds diving in courtship displays and found that they reached
a maximum velocity of about 385 body lengths per second, "the
highest known length-specific velocity attained by any vertebrate." He calculated their actual speed at sixty-one miles per
hour (27.3 meters per second), but in relation to body length, it
is faster than the space shuttle reentering the atmosphere at a
mere 207 body lengths per second. Peregrine Falcons are said to

be the fastest flyers, but a Peregrine diving at top speed is moving at only 200 body lengths per second.

Measuring such rapid movement became possible only with the development of high-speed photography and the electronic flash. In the late 1950s, Crawford H. Greenewalt, the former president of Du Pont Chemical Company who was also an artist and a naturalist with a serious interest in hummingbirds, took hundreds of high-speed motion pictures of female Ruby-throated Hummingbirds in order to learn how fast their wings beat and how they hovered. Greenewalt developed a method to capture the wing motion on film with a camera of his own design, supplemented by bulky equipment and spare parts that weighed in total approximately 250 pounds. His equipment produced a short, bright electronic flash that froze the hummingbird's wing in flight, and he set it up so that when a hummingbird flew into a beam of light that was aimed at a photocell, it automatically tripped the camera's shutter—the bird took its own picture. He also motorized the shutter so that every time the flash went off the film was advanced. By slowing the speed of the projector, he could see each up- and downstroke of the bird's wings, and knowing the elapsed time of the film enabled him to calculate the number of wing beats per second. The result was a huge portfolio of beautiful photographs as well as an enriched understanding of hummingbird flight. Modern digital versions of this equipment using pulsating lasers make the task even easier and much more precise.

Question 2: How does a hummingbird hover?

Answer: Hummingbirds have a unique wing design and an enlarged heart, both of which facilitate their ability to hover. They also have anatomical features that make them especially light: air sacs in hollow bones and body cavities, and only one ovary in the female. Because hovering is metabolically costly, their high metabolism is another important factor, because they are so small and rapidly lose body heat (see Chapter 2, Question 8: How can hummingbirds be so active?).

Hummingbirds expend thousands of calories when they hover for extended periods, and they use a large portion of their energy hovering while they gather *more* food to meet their exhaustive energy needs, maneuvering in all directions to insert their bill into hundreds or thousands of windblown flowers every day. Their agile hovering gives them an evolutionary advantage, allowing them to remain stationary in space while they feed for up to 90 percent of their flight time, according to Douglas Wylie of the University of Alberta.

Only hummingbirds can hover for long periods of time. A few other birds are transient hoverers—Ospreys, some hawks, warblers, kestrels, kingfishers, and some passerines can remain stationary briefly—but only hummingbirds can fly backward, up, down, and side to side. They can even fly upside down briefly by doing a backward summersault. Hovering is best viewed in slow motion, as in the educational video by Thomas Kaminski (see references). A hummingbird's wings do not beat up and down as you might expect, but instead move forward and backward with the wing actually upside down momentarily, so that the tip of the wing makes a horizontal figure eight (see figure 10).

Lift is generated on both the forward and the backward stroke and the rapid movement of the wings permits the bird to remain stationary. The bird is able to shift from this position in any direction by slight adjustments in the angle and movement of the wings. Scientists have recently used microscopic droplets of olive oil and a pulsating laser to photograph the movement of air created by the wings of a hovering Rufous Hummingbird. Using a piece of equipment called a digital particle imaging velocimeter, Douglas Warrick and colleagues learned that a hummingbird produces 75 percent of the lift needed to support its weight on the forward or downstroke of its wings, and 25 percent on the back or upstroke. In some hummingbird species, expanding and contracting the tail feathers or pumping the tail may further facilitate hovering.

A hummingbird's wing bones are relatively stronger than those of other birds, and the hand part of the wing is longer and the arm part of the wing is shorter. The joint between the upper

Figure 10. A hovering female Rufous Hummingbird *Selasphorus rufus*. Here she has completed her forward or downstroke and is turning her wing over to begin the back or upstroke. By turning the wing over, she gains lift on the backstroke.

arm bone (humerus) and the shoulder is a more pronounced ball-and-socket joint than is found in other birds, allowing the wing to swivel 180 degrees at the shoulder. The muscles that beat the wings are large and strong and can move the wings very rapidly for extended periods of time. A hummingbird's flight (pectoral) muscles account for more than 25 percent of its total body weight, compared to only about 5 percent for the pectoral muscles of an average person.

Douglas Wylie and Andrew Iwaniuk of the University of Alberta tried to determine how hummingbirds can remain stationary while their rapid wing-beat rhythm (in addition to the wind) would seem to jostle them and jerk them around. They found that stability during hovering is dependent on the optokinetic response (OKR) generated in a particular nucleus in the brain.

The OKR stabilizes the visual field or gaze. As Wylie explained in an interview in *Nature:* "If you want to make sure you stay stationary, you just have to make sure nothing on the retina moves. That's what this nucleus does." In comparison with its relative size in thirty-seven species of birds that Wylie and colleagues examined, this area of the brain in nine hummingbird species was significantly larger. The species studied that are transient hoverers also showed some degree of enlargement, but it was not comparable to the relative size of the area in hummingbirds. The researchers plan further studies to investigate how this area reacts to visual motion.

Question 3: How is the hummingbird's skeleton adapted to the bird's lifestyle?

Answer: The hummingbird skeleton is a reflection of the hummingbird's flying ability and its feeding habits. Some of the bones are hollow to reduce weight and to provide space for air sacs that are part of these birds' efficient respiratory system. The skull is large in relation to the whole body, and the relatively large brain meets the birds' needs to remember where to find food and where to go when they migrate. They also need to see the environment accurately to find food and to escape predation (see Chapter 2, Question 1: Are hummingbirds intelligent?).

The cervical (neck) vertebrae, the only elements of the spinal column that are easily moveable, allow a hummingbird to move its head around to feed, preen, give food to the nestlings, collect nesting material, and fight rivals. The first vertebra below the skull has a single pivot point or joint with the skull that allows a hummingbird to turn its head left and right 180 degrees so that it can see behind itself. (Mammals have two joints between the skull and first cervical vertebra, making it impossible to move the head as far laterally as birds can.)

All the rest of the vertebrae, from the thoracic (chest), lumbar (back), and sacrum (lower back), are fused into a single bone called the synsacrum; the pelvic bones are also fused. The synsacrum and the fused vertebrae keep the body rigid as the

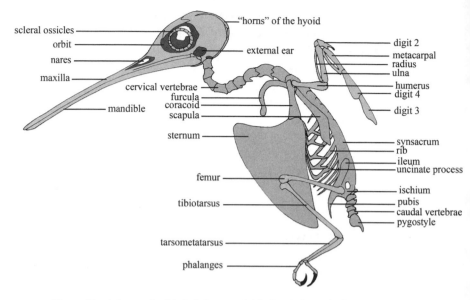

Figure 11. A hummingbird skeleton, which shows how the bone structure supports the bird's lifestyle. The large sternum holds the powerful wing muscles. The short, strong arm and the long hand together support the flight feathers. The legs are reduced, as they are used only for perching; the skull is large to hold the large brain and large eyes; and the bill is elongated so the bird can probe flowers for nectar.

bird flies, making it unnecessary for the bird to have the added weight of muscles and ligaments to keep it stable. The ribs are larger in relation to body size than the ribs of a mammal, and they have hook-shaped, bony spurs (uncinate processes) that overlap other ribs to keep the rib cage stable as well. The caudal vertebrae at the base of the tail are almost inflexible, but they allow the bird to move its tail from side to side or up and down. Hummingbirds can move their tail feathers as a group to fan them out, but they cannot move each one individually.

The wing bones in the upper arm (humerus) and the lower arm (radius and ulna) are short, but the hand bones that include the wrist (metacarpals) and fingers (digits or phalanges) are relatively long in hummingbirds, keeping the wing stiff. The large sternum or breastbone serves as a stable attachment for the giant flight muscles that account for more than 26 percent of a hummingbird's body weight, among the highest percentage in birds. The two major flight muscles are the pectoralis major that pulls the wings down and the supracoracoideus that pulls the wings up. Both muscles are attached to the humerus, the upper arm bone, and the supracoracoideus muscle and its tendon go up and over the coracoid bone at the shoulder to pull the wing up, acting like a pulley on the shoulder. Imagine these two muscles, one on top of the other, contracting alternately eighty times a second to pull the humerus up and down so the bird can hover. Think of the heat this must produce—not only metabolic heat but also friction between the muscle's sheaths and the tendon moving so rapidly through a canal in the shoulder joint!

Birds' legs are similar to mammalian legs, except biologists have learned that the ankle and foot bones have moved around and fused with the lower long bones of the leg. The phalanges (digits or toes) are similar to those of humans, except that hummingbirds have only four toes, three facing forward made up of three bones each, and one facing backward made up of only one long bone and a terminal claw. In hummingbirds, the legs are rather weak, as the feet are used only for perching, working around the nest, and fighting (see Chapter 2, Question 12: Can hummingbirds walk?).

Question 4: How many feathers does a hummingbird have?

Answer: Depending on the species, a hummingbird has from about nine hundred to as many as seventeen hundred feathers. Because the birds are so small, they have the fewest feathers of any group of birds. A swan, in comparison, may have more than twenty-five thousand feathers.

There are six types of feathers, most of which are present on larger birds but only three of which are obvious on a hummingbird: body or contour feathers that cover the head, back, sides, breast, and belly of the bird; flight feathers that make up the

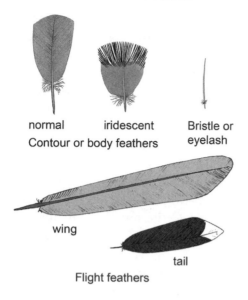

normal   iridescent   Bristle or
Contour or body feathers   eyelash

wing

tail

Flight feathers

Figure 12. An adult hummingbird's three types of feathers: flight feathers (wing and tail), contour feathers (body), and bristles or lashes around the eyes and bill.

wing and tail; and bristle feathers around the eyes and bill (see figure 12). Birds have the ability to raise (fluff up) and lower (flatten) body feathers using the tiny muscles attached to each feather papilla (the bump from which a feather grows).

The flight feathers of the wing—called remiges, from the Latin for "oarsman"—are ten primaries and three to six secondary feathers. Most small songbirds have nine primaries, and more primitive birds have ten or twelve. The primaries provide most of the lift and power of the wings for flight and are counted from the inside out; they arise from the hand of the bird (see figure 13). Hummingbirds have three to six secondary flight feathers that are smaller and arise from the arm of the wing. In comparison, an albatross has thirty-two secondaries, and one species of eagle has thirty-five.

Most species of hummingbirds have only ten tail feathers (rectrices; singular rectrix). By comparison, most birds have twelve, although some songbirds have only six and some seabirds have as many as thirty-two. The feathers on a hummingbird's wings and tail that border and slightly overlap the bases of its flight feathers are contour feathers called coverts; they cover the base of the flight feathers in an arrangement of primary and secondary coverts. The coverts on the arm are in three layers—the greater, median, and lesser coverts. The tail has undertail and uppertail coverts as well.

The only other feather type on a hummingbird includes the very tiny bristles or eyelash feathers, which may have a few downy barbs at the base and then only a shaft—like a hair—projecting outward. They are found around the eyes and often around the mouth. Most other birds have down feathers under their body feathers, semiplumes (down at the base and contour shaped at the tip), or filoplumes (a long shaft with no barbs and a few downy barbs at the tip), but hummingbirds do not.

The feathers of hummingbirds, like those of all other birds, grow in finite areas called tracts or pterylae (see figure 14). Their location in hummingbirds was mapped for the first time in 1906 by Hubert L. Clark. If you have a hummingbird in your hand, you can blow the feathers apart and see bare skin in many places (see figure 32). Since the feathers that cover the hummingbird's

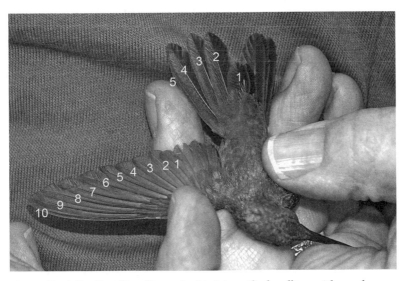

Figure 13. A live Berylline Hummingbird *Amazilia beryllina,* with numbers indicating the flight feathers on the right wing and right half of the tail.

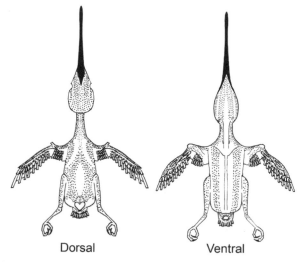

Dorsal   Ventral

Figure 14. Dorsal (back) and ventral (front) views show how feathers grow in tracts and not all over the body of the typical hummingbird. The wing and tail flight feathers are shown as pinfeather sheathes, while the contour (body) feathers arise from papillae, shown as black dots.

breast and belly grow from areas on the side of the body, and because the skin is very thin, you can see body fat deposited below the skin prior to migration, and you can see developing eggs in the female. Birds that evolved earlier than hummingbirds, such as the ostrich, emu, and penguin, have very wide pterylae so that their feathers appear to be spread more evenly over the whole body.

Question 5: How do birds keep their feathers so smooth and their wing feathers in perfect shape?

Answer: Preening is a bird's way of cleaning itself, searching and removing debris and parasites and adjusting its feathers to keep them all in line. When birds preen, they may fluff feathers in one tract at a time, and sometimes you can see the bare spaces between the tracts.

Feathers are made of a protein called keratin, the same substance that forms fingernails. The feathers grow from bumps (papillae) in the feather tracts (pterylae) much as human hair grows. However, a feather is far more complicated than a hair, and the structure that keeps the feathers smooth and the wing feathers relatively rigid can be seen only with a microscope. The developing feather grows in a sheath that appears as a whitish rod (called "pinfeathers" on domestic chickens). If you were to pull out a pinfeather of a living bird, it would bleed, because the papillae are filled with blood, which brings keratin and nutrients to the developing feather. Once the feather is completely formed, the papilla shrinks and the blood vessels atrophy—the feather is now dead, containing no living tissue. If you cut a feather with scissors or if a bird damages a feather, it will not grow back. However, if you pull out a feather, a new one will grow in its place.

Each flight or contour feather is made up of a central shaft (rachis) and a vane. The vane is made up of barbs that branch out on both sides of the shaft. Each barb has microscopic barbules that project outward on both sides of the barb. The proximal barbules are those closest to the bird's body, and distal barbules are the ones farthest from the body. The proximal barbules are usually like thorns—medium-length, sharp-pointed extensions—while the distal barbules are longer and have many tiny hooks that lock with the proximal barbules on the next barb like Velcro or a hook and loop fastener (see figure 15).

While preening, birds can relock the barbules to keep the feather vane intact. They run their bill over the feather and arrange the barbs so that the barbules have a chance to get in place and lock onto each other, which makes the feather rigid. When all the barbules are hooked, the feather makes a perfect oar or paddle for flight, strong enough to hold its shape when the bird creates a downward force of the wing against the air that gives the bird lift. At the same time, the feather is somewhat flexible and bends when necessary, especially at the tip or when the bird is moving through branches and bumps its wings on twigs.

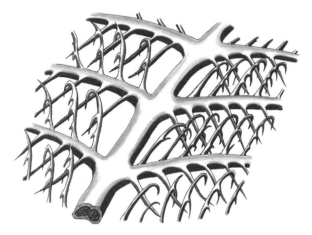

Figure 15. Structure of flight feathers and most body feathers, with a central shaft (rachis) with barbs on either side. The hooked distal barbules (those away from the body) of one barb mesh with the proximal barbules (those nearest the body) on the next barb to hold the feather together.

Question 6: When do hummingbirds molt?

Answer: Molting is the replacement of worn feathers with new ones, and different species of birds have different molt cycles. Some birds molt twice a year to change their drab basic winter plumage for their colorful breeding or summer plumage. In many species a series of molt cycles during the first years of life changes the plumage bit by bit annually until the adult plumage is achieved. Bald Eagles, for example, take about five years to reach the full adult plumage of dark brown body and pure white head and tail.

Hummingbirds' lives are relatively short; they do not have time to wait five years to reach full adult breeding plumage. Because molting takes a great deal of energy and requires lots of protein to make all the new feathers, hummingbirds molt only once a year, thus conserving energy for their rapid and costly lifestyle. Once most species of hummingbirds molt their juvenile plumage (the first feathers grown after hatching) and grow a new set of feathers, they have reached their adult plumage, and each successive annual molt will simply replace the color and style of the feathers they have dropped. In a few of the larger hummingbird species, it may be possible to determine that a bird is in its second year of life by examining its feathers because the first annual postjuvenile molt does not always result in full adult plumage. For example, a male Magnificent Hummingbird returning north from Mexico to Arizona for the first time, after being hatched the previous summer, may have more gray-white tips in the tail feathers, remnants of a juvenile tail; the green gorget may be only half feathered; and the purple crown may extend from the back of the head only halfway to the base of the bill.

Because molting, breeding, and migration are all energy-consuming processes, these demanding activities usually overlap as little as possible. In general the annual molt cycle of most hummingbirds occurs after the breeding season is over, earlier for males than for females because the males' duties are done after the females are fertilized (see Chapter 4, Question 9: Do both hummingbird parents take care of the nest?). Some adults and juveniles may start to molt while still in the nesting area, but most do not molt until they have safely migrated to their wintering grounds. Usually the complete annual molt takes several months, and it can be delayed until the birds are back on the breeding grounds in the spring (this is true of many male Broad-tailed Hummingbirds).

In some tropical species that live near the equator, when food resources are scarce and energy is in short supply, molting or breeding may be delayed. These birds have no need to migrate because the climatic conditions remain relatively constant throughout the year, so for them there is no predictable time for breeding or an annual molt. While they may not breed if food resources are particularly short, we suspect that they do replace all their feathers annually.

Molting usually begins with the body feathers, except for the brilliantly colored feathers of males. The male's bright iridescent gorget and head feathers are usually replaced last, just before courting commences, ensuring that these feathers, so important for obtaining a mate and defending territory, are in their best condition. The flight feathers are molted in sequence in trochilids from number 1 closest to the body to number 8, then 10, and finally primary 9, but in hermits sequentially from number 1 to 10.

Usually one or two primaries are molted at the same time, and then they grow almost all the way in before the next primary is lost, a system that seems to best preserve flight maneuverability. The rectrices (tail feathers) are usually molted from the inside out, but the sequence varies. Usually rectrix number 5 (the outermost) is molted before numbers 3 and/or 4. The molt of both wing and tail feathers is bilaterally symmetrical to retain the bird's flight balance.

Question 7: Are all hummingbirds brilliantly colored?

Answer: Most male hummingbirds have evolved a wide array of brilliantly colored plumages, usually on the head and neck, but sometimes on the whole underside of the bird, on portions of the wings and tail, and on the back (see color plates). These colorful males belong to the subfamily Trochilinae, and even in this subfamily, males of some species are very dull, as are most female hummingbirds and male and female hermits (Phaethornithinae), members of the other subfamily of hummingbirds (see Chapter 1, Question 5: How are hummingbirds classified?). Hermits live primarily in deep tropical forests where sunlight usually does not penetrate, so iridescent feathers would serve no visual purpose as they would not shine (see this chapter, Question 8: What are iridescent feathers?).

The back of a trochilid hummingbird is typically a shade of green, although there are a few exceptions. Most of the dorsal feathers are iridescent, but the basic green color is a result of a yellow pigment and iridescent feathers that reflect blue. The combination of yellow and blue makes the feather appear green, and even when a hummingbird is flying away or across in front of you, you will see a flash of green as the bird passes through a patch of sunlight. The brilliant color signals the bird's presence,

Descriptive Hummingbird Names

In this list of the common names of hummingbirds, you can see that the people who first identified and described the species tried to come up with descriptive names related to the feather patterns or shapes and colors of the bird. Some of these common names are used in several different genera.

Avocetbill	Jewelfront	Sicklebill
Awlbill	Lancebill	Snowcap
Barbthroat	Magnificent	Spatuletail
Black-chinned	Mango	Starthroat
Blossomcrown	Metaltail	Streamertail
Brilliant	Mountaineer	Sunangel
Comet	Piedtail	Sunbeam
Coquette	Plovercrest	Sungem
Coronet	Plumeleteer	Thornbill
Emerald	Puffleg	Topaz
Fairy	Racket-tail	Trainbearer
Firecrown	Ruby-throated	Velvetbreast
Goldenthroat	Sabrewing	Violet-ear
Helmetcrest	Sapphire	Whitetip
Hillstar	Sapphirewing	Woodnymph
Inca	Sheartail	Woodstar
Jacobin		

and this signal can be used to threaten birds that invade its feeding areas and to keep rival males away from a female. Males also display their colors to attract a mate, and each species' unique coloration is what we use to help identify them to species.

Females normally are duller in color than males in almost all species of birds, an advantage that makes them less conspicuous to predators while on the nest incubating and brooding young. Dull colors are also an advantage for young birds still in the nest when the female is absent, as well as for those just fledged and not practiced in rapid escape flight to avoid predators. Not to be completely outdone by the males, most trochilid humming-bird females have some iridescent feathers on the back, and some have patches or individual spangles of iridescent feathers on the throat. In some species, females always have some iridescent feathers, but we have seen some Anna's Hummingbirds that have a number of large, malelike spangles (iridescent feathers) on the throat, and some with iridescent red feathers on the crown. Whether this is related to changing hormone levels is unknown.

Question 8: What are iridescent feathers?

Answer: Iridescent feathers are those that shine brightly in sunlight and often change color depending on the angle at which you look at them. Each flight or contour feather has a central shaft and a vane that consists of barbs that branch out on both sides of the shaft. Microscopic barbules project outwards on both sides of the barb, usually ending with hooks that connect the feathers. Most iridescent feathers are small, usually only about one-quarter inch long. Only the distal third of the feather (toward the tip) is structured to be iridescent, and this portion of the feather is the only part that shows when all the feathers are aligned on the bird's body. While the base of an iridescent feather is flat, like other noniridescent body or contour feathers, its distal third has no hooks and therefore the tip is relatively loose. The distal barbules of the iridescent part of the feather contain melanin pigment that makes them look gray, brown, black, yellow, or (rarely) green when there is no bright light shining on them. They appear iridescent only when light shines on them at certain angles.

The iridescent color is not the result of pigment absorption and reflection as in noniridescent feathers. Instead, it is like the colors in a soap bubble, depending on light being passed through a substance that is different than air and being partially reflected back. The barbules of the iridescent part of the feather contain microscopic plates with elliptical air bubbles between them, and the amount of air in the bubbles creates dif-

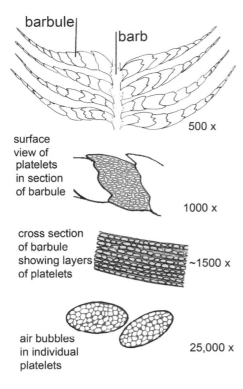

barbule

barb

surface
view of
platelets
in section
of barbule

500 x

1000 x

cross section
of barbule
showing layers
of platelets

~1500 x

air bubbles
in individual
platelets

25,000 x

Figure 16. Barbules of iridescent feathers, each section containing eight to ten layers of platelets interspersed with layers of pigment. The combination of the pigment and layers of air-filled platelets refracts light in different wavelengths, producing the colors we see.

ferent refractive indices that produce different colors depending on the angle of light hitting the feather and the position of the viewer. So the throat (gorget) of a male Magnificent Hummingbird may appear bright apple green, aquamarine, or black, and the gorget and crown of a male Anna's Hummingbird may appear rose red, golden, or black. Black or a very dark color is always one color option due to the melanin pigment that sometimes shows through.

Question 9: If I find a hummingbird feather, what can it tell me?

Answer: When you find a feather, you can easily tell whether it is a flight feather or a body feather. Body or contour feathers are softer and more flexible than the flight feathers from the wings and tail, so if the feather is stiff and the barbs seem to be tightly locked, it is a flight feather. If the vane is about the same size on both the left and right side of the shaft, it is probably either a secondary wing feather or a tail feather. If it is a primary wing feather, it will be slightly bent or curved so that one of the flat sides is convex and the other concave. Turn the feather so that the convex side is up; that is the top of the wing. To tell which wing the feather came from, you can observe that (usually) one half of the feather is wider than the other half, for example, the vane on the left side of the shaft is wider than the vane on the right. If you hold the base of the shaft in your hand with the feather pointing away from you, if the left vane is wider than the right, the feather came from the bird's left wing.

FOUR

Reproduction

Question 1: How does a hummingbird attract a mate?

Answer: Many hummingbird species are dimorphic, meaning that the male and female have different plumages, with the female generally being less colorful. The males use the bright, iridescent plumage on the gorget, crown, or front of their body to attract a mate. Many species have specially developed tail feathers or a crest on the head that may serve to convince a female that this male is a stronger and more fit mate than his competition.

James Clark of the University of California, Berkeley, filmed Anna's Hummingbirds performing courtship displays, and he noted that they orient the display dive in relation to the sun, so that they "look like a little magenta fireball dropping out of the sky." This extreme behavior offers the brightest possible image to a receptive female in order to chase her to her nesting area so they can mate. Males fly up high and typically plunge ten or fifteen times in a row toward the female. Clark's analysis of the dives indicates that their maximum speed reaches about 385 body lengths per second, making them the world's fastest bird. When they pull up to stop the dive, they experience a pull that is nine times the force of gravity, matched only by the speed of a jet fighter pilot doing aerial maneuvers. The birds can survive this incredible speed without trauma only because they maintain it for less than 0.3 seconds.

In many North American hummingbird species, males approach perched females with loud chattering or other vocal sounds. In mating behavior that was first described by Stephen Russell, a hummingbird research ornithologist from the University of Arizona, the female leads the male into the area where she has constructed her nest; when she perches, the male may attempt to copulate or, if the female is not ready, he may begin emitting loud courtship calls and/or initiate a shuttle display (see figure 17). The female may follow the actions of the male, pointing at him with her bill, but if she is not ready or decides not to mate, she flies away. In some cases, an aggressive male tries to compel a less receptive female to copulate by forcing her to the ground (see also this chapter, Question 4: How do hummingbirds reproduce?).

Males of many hermit species (usually less conspicuously colored), as well as some brightly colored trochilids, gather in groups, called leks, where they sing and display for females that visit the lek to choose a mate. Male animals of many species gather in a lek to attract females, including some other birds, some insects, certain fish, some bats, and other mammals. A

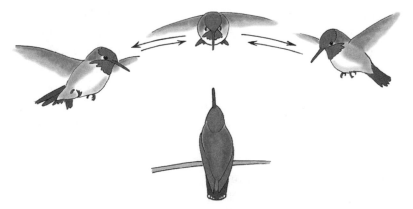

Figure 17. Diagram of the shuttle display of a male Anna's Hummingbird *Calypte anna*. The bird hovers, moving left and right in a short arc above the female.

few examples of the extensive research on the behavior of hummingbirds in leks will give you an idea of what may occur.

Marco Pizo and Wesley Silva observed that Swallow-tailed Hummingbirds *Eupetomena macroura* in Sao Paolo, Brazil, gather in groups of from six to fifteen individuals and sing together briefly before and after sunrise. Sooty-capped Hermits *Phaethornis augusti*, studied by Carol Ramjohn and her colleagues in Venezuela, collected in smaller groups. While they are in the lek, they sing approximately 75 percent of the time, mostly in the early morning and late afternoon. Green Hermits *Phaethornis guy* observed by Elizabeth MacDougall-Shackleton and Heidi Harbison in Panama formed leks of about a dozen males that sing in subgroups, spending more time singing if they are near the center of the lek. Sandra Gaunt of Ohio State University found that male Green Violet-ears *Colibri thalassinus* sing so cooperatively that from a distance it sounds as if only one bird is singing. This fascinating phenomenon demonstrates a highly organized method of attracting a mate. Leks are probably more popular among hermits because they lack the colorful plumage with which to attract the attention of females, so they use their voices in a dramatic way.

Question 2: How do hummingbirds protect their mating territory?

Answer: During the mating season, male hummingbirds do all they can to drive away competing males. The defending male uses loud noises, threatening postures, and aggressive actions to scare off rivals and any other birds that invade its feeding or courtship territory. The male sings, perched in an exposed position with gorget and crown feathers ruffled and the head turned upward at a 45-degree angle. If an intruder approaches, the bird lowers his head and increases the intensity and speed of his song. If the intruder does not leave, a chase will probably follow.

Some males use the chatter-sway threat posture to defend their territory. With his tail spread to make him look larger, the bird perches facing an intruder, and swings his head from side to side while loudly chattering. Males may also use a dramatic dive display to intimidate unwanted visitors (see figure 18). Stephen Russell described the approximately twelve-second dive display of the Anna's Hummingbird, which begins with the bird hovering from six to thirteen feet (two to four meters) in front of the hummingbird or person who is the object of the display. Next, the bird flies straight up more than one hundred feet, then "plummets in a near-vertical dive from the top of the climb, and ends with an explosive squeak within half a meter" of the

Figure 18. Diagram of the dive display of a male Anna's Hummingbird *Calypte anna,* also used by other species. The bird rises slowly, often moving back and forth, then dives toward the intruder. The male Anna's makes a loud chirp with its tail feathers at the bottom of the dive.

Figure 19. Foot of a Black-chinned Hummingbird *Archilochus alexandri*, showing the sharp claws that can be used in fighting other hummingbirds.

object of the display. The squeak or chirp at the end of the dive display is made by the tail feathers (see Chapter 2, Question 17: Do hummingbirds sing?).

Hummingbirds have been seen using their sharp claws to fight off another bird, and fighting males in a territorial battle can severely injure each other. We have seen male hummingbirds with scars in the breast muscles that we assume were caused by having been stabbed by another male. Dead hummingbirds have been found with another dead hummingbird's bill implanted in the breast muscle. Most of these aggressive behaviors occur when one or both birds are flying, and they are usually preceded by vocal threats and posturing that has failed to drive the other bird away.

Question 3: Are hummingbirds monogamous?

Answer: Almost all hummingbirds are polygynous, which means that one male may mate with several females. In some species a female may mate with more than one male (polyandry). When both sexes typically have multiple partners, the association is called polygynandrous. The degree to which species mate with multiple partners has rarely been studied because it requires marking wild birds and being able to observe them for long periods during the mating season. In all species studied so far, no pair bond is established that lasts beyond the very brief courtship and actual mating, and the total time the pair is together may be only a minute or two.

Question 4: How do hummingbirds reproduce?

Answer: Hummingbirds reproduce the same way all other birds and all other vertebrates do. The male releases sperm into the female's vent, the genital opening that contains an internal sac called a cloaca. If she is ready to copulate, she will twist her tail downward and spread it slightly, fluttering her wings to keep balanced on her perch. Both birds have to cooperate as the male flutters on the back of the female and twists his abdomen and tail so that their genital openings make contact—his is also called a vent. The male does not have a penis, but he injects a package of sperm from his cloaca into the female's cloaca in what is called a cloacal kiss. The sperm swim up the female's oviduct, and one spermatozoan fertilizes the ovum (egg) as it is released from the ovary. The word "cloaca" comes from the Latin word that means "sewer," and it is used to describe this posterior receptacle at the end of the large intestine in most birds, reptiles, and amphibians from which they also excrete both urine and feces.

Question 5: Can hummingbirds of one species mate with those of another species?

Answer: In the species that breed in North America it is relatively common to find hummingbird hybrids, the results of the male of one species having fertilized the egg of a bird of a different species—even of another genus. Apparently the urge to

mate is so strong that a male who cannot easily locate a female
of his own species will court a female of another species. The
same instinctive desire to reproduce exists in females, inclining
them to be receptive to a male of a different species.

Banders report many hybrid hummingbirds, but often the
parentage of the bird is not obvious. In most cases, the hybrid
is an F1 generation, which means both parents are full-blooded
species. But it may be possible for an F1 bird to mate with a full
species or with another F1, producing an F2 generation whose
parentage is even more difficult to determine. Virtually all the
common North American breeding species of hummingbirds
have been reported to have hybridized with one or more of the
other species, but, according to Josep del Hoyo, most hybrids
occur in the genera *Calypte, Archilochus,* and *Selasphorus.* Hybridization is also suspected in hermits but no documentation is yet
available, and we do not know if the offspring of these hybrids
are fertile.

Question 6: How big is a hummingbird's egg?

Answer: Hummingbirds lay the smallest eggs in the avian
world. The size of the egg is related to the body size of the female. The smallest hummingbird, the Bee Hummingbird of
Cuba, lays elliptical or oval eggs that are about three-eighths
of an inch long (11 by 8 millimeters) and weigh only 0.4 grams
(1 gram equals about 0.035 ounces). The Giant Hummingbird of
the Andes lays much larger eggs, three-quarters of an inch long
(20 by 12 millimeters), weighing 1.4 grams. The smallest North
American hummingbird for which we have data, the Calliope
Hummingbird, lays eggs that are about half the size of a jelly-
bean and weigh less than half a gram. Anna's Hummingbirds

Figure 20. The two-egg clutch of a Black-
chinned Hummingbird *Archilochus alexandri* compared to a dime (actual size).

Formation and Content of the Hummingbird Egg

The hummingbird egg is a miniature version of the familiar chicken egg; there is a shell, a white, and a yolk. The yolk is pale yellow to almost white, the albumin is clear or cloudy white, and the shell is pale white. The egg (or ovum) forms in the bird's ovary, and once it is fertilized it passes down the oviduct. The oviduct secretes all the albumin and shell materials in layers until the egg is ready to be laid, in about twenty-four hours (see Chapter 4, Question 4: How do hummingbirds reproduce?).

The yolk of the egg contains the ovum, and the female's diet of nectar and insects provides proteins and lipids that form alternating light and dark layers of yolk material. The dark layer contains more fat and it is laid down during the day, while the light layers contain more protein and are produced at night. In the center of the yolk is a lighter-colored sphere of protein called the latebra, and a narrow column of this same material extends to the outer edge of the yolk where the tiny blastodisc floats. The blastodisc contains the genetic material (zygote) and tissue that will begin to divide to form the embryo. The yolk will eventually be contained in the gut of the embryo to provide nutrition for its development. A membrane around the yolk extends into the albumin from the opposite ends of the yolk. It has twisted strands called the chalazae that extend outward through the albumin to the outer egg ligament.

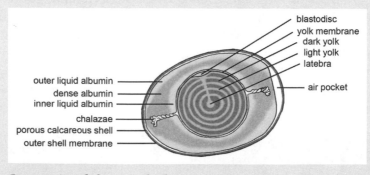

Cross-section of a hummingbird egg.

Formation and Content of the Hummingbird Egg

Outside the yolk membrane are three layers of albumin—the inner layer is a liquid, next is a layer of dense albumin, and finally there is an outer liquid layer. The albumin is primarily protein that acts as a cushion for the developing egg and allows the yolk and developing embryo to rotate, using the chalazae as an axis, when the female hummingbird moves the egg around in the nest. The albumin has some bactericidal properties and also provides some nutrition for the embryo.

The embryo creates a chorioallantoic membrane that eventually surrounds the albumin next to the shell. Many microscopic pores in the eggshell allow the embryo to breathe, and air concentrates in a pocket at one end of the egg between this membrane and the shell. The membrane is rich in capillaries and permits the embryo to take up nutrients from the yolk and albumin, deposit wastes, and breathe from the air space. The air pocket gets larger as the developing embryo consumes the albumin and yolk.

Protecting this complex arrangement is the egg's shell. To create it, the female has to find a source of calcium, consume it, and convert it from a solid to a state that can pass through her intestinal membrane to be carried along in her bloodstream to the oviduct, where the calcium is deposited to form the shell.

lay slightly larger eggs that weigh about half a gram, roughly 12 percent of the female's body weight. The Magnificent Hummingbird, a larger bird, lays eggs that weigh almost one gram, in roughly the same proportion to the female's body weight.

Question 7: How many young do hummingbirds have each year?

Answer: Females normally lay two eggs, the second following the first in twenty-four to forty-eight hours. On the rare occasion that a female lays only one egg, it might be because there

Hummingbird Nest with Six Eggs

A female Anna's Hummingbird built a nest right outside a window of Mary Estrada's house in Goodyear, Arizona, just west of Phoenix, and the bird (she assumes it's the same bird) has returned to the nest every year for the past three years. Mary holds a large mirror over the nest when the bird is away so she can see the eggs and young birds as they mature.

In each of the first two years, the bird laid two eggs, incubated them, and raised the young until they finally left the nest. In the third year, 2008, the bird returned and laid two eggs in March. After two weeks, the eggs were still intact when Mary checked, although they should have hatched in about that length of time. In early April she checked again, and now there were four eggs in the nest. She waited two more weeks, and the four eggs remained. In early May she found the original four eggs still there, lightly covered with nesting material,

Nest containing six eggs laid by a single Anna's Hummingbird *Calypte anna*. This unique photograph was taken using a mirror suspended over the bird's nest. (*Photograph courtesy of Mary K. Estrada*)

Hummingbird Nest with Six Eggs

with two more eggs laid on top of them, for a total of six eggs on which the female was still sitting. After another two weeks, the female abandoned the nest. None of the six eggs hatched.

Hummingbirds normally lay two eggs per clutch, spaced one to two days apart. A greater number of eggs in a single nest is usually the result of more than one female laying eggs in the same nest. If eggs do not hatch, it is usually because they aren't fertile or the embryo has died from a lack of heat needed from incubation. In this case, there was evidence the female incubated the eggs from the start, so we assume the cause of the failure to hatch was the eggs not being fertile. Either the female never mated with a male and laid eggs anyway—unlikely in the hummingbird world, where the males are highly aggressive—or the female's ova were incapable of being fertilized and forming an embryo. We expect it is possible for a female to have passed the age when she is able to lay fertilizable eggs because of hormonal changes that may occur in older birds. We know estrogen is required to maintain female plumage, and if estrogen is depleted, the plumage may return to more male-like colors. Rarely, we have seen adult females that have large red spangles in the gorget and some red feathers on the crown where they are not supposed to be, and this male-like coloring could be the result of depleted estrogen, overbalanced by testosterone. No hormonal studies have been done to our knowledge on hummingbirds of increasing age, but this is an interesting area for future research.

are not enough nutrients available in the area to produce a second egg. If there are more than two eggs in a nest, it is thought that one egg of the first clutch either did not hatch or was laid by a different female (a process called egg dumping).

The two eggs in a clutch are usually about the same size. If the second egg is smaller than the first, it is probably the result of insufficient nutrients due to fewer flowers and insects in

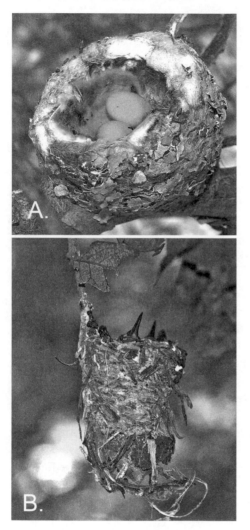

Figure 21. *A:* Black-chinned Hummingbird *Archilochus alexandri* nest with a typical two-egg clutch. The nest is made of plant fiber cemented together with spider silk. Lichens added to the outside make the nest blend with the surrounding vegetation; the inside is lined with soft plant down. (*Photograph courtesy of Harold Greeney*); *B:* an unusual two-tiered nest of a Broad-billed Hummingbird *Cynanthus latirostris,* with a newer nest built on top of an older nest. Two young birds wait to be fed.

the area. If the first clutch is lost to predation or weather (wind and rain can destroy a nest), the female usually attempts to nest again and produce a second clutch. In some areas, especially in the southern United States, a female lays a second clutch after the first set of youngsters has fledged. She may reconstruct the same nest, make another nest nearby using parts of the old one, or start a new nest from scratch.

William Baltosser, then at New Mexico State University, studied the reasons for nest failure in southwestern New Mexico and southeastern Arizona from 1976 to 1980. He reported that nearly 80 percent of all failed nest attempts were due to predation—the majority as a result of predation on the eggs and the rest because of predation on the nestlings. Failures as a result of structural problems with the nest, abandonment by the mother, or infertility were low. On average during the years of his study, the number of young that fledged (successfully left the nest) per female ranged from 0.16 for Costa's Hummingbirds to 1.16 for Black-chinned and Magnificent Hummingbirds, 1.43 for Violet-crowned Hummingbirds, and 2.32 for Broad-billed Hummingbirds. These results are consistent with previous studies, according to Baltosser.

Question 8: How long does it take for hummingbird eggs to hatch?

Answer: The incubation period, which is the time it takes for the eggs to hatch after being laid, is from sixteen to nineteen days in most North American species, but in Central America the time may shorten to fourteen days, probably because of the warmer ambient temperatures. In the Andes Mountains of South America the incubation time often extends to more than twenty-two days, with a maximum of forty days, according to del Hoyo. The differences are probably due to colder temperatures in the mountains, and to the necessity for the mother bird to spend more time off the nest foraging. When the average temperature of the eggs is lower, they develop more slowly.

Question 9: Do both hummingbird parents take care of the nest?

Answer: No, only the female takes care of nesting duties. She constructs the nest, lays the eggs, incubates the eggs, and feeds the young until they are on their own. The only roles males play in reproduction are courtship and mating.

Question 10: Why are hummingbird nests so hard to find?

Answer: Hummingbirds are expert designers, individually decorating each nest to match its surroundings (usually a tree) to help hide it. Trochilid hummingbirds decorate their nests with bits of moss, bark, lichen, and grass to camouflage it. The whole nest is bound together with spider webbing that allows the nest to expand in size as the young hummingbirds grow. Hummingbird nests are very small, hidden under leaves and often high above human eye level, and many predators have trouble finding them. Hermits that nest in the tropics build nests on the back of palm fronds or *Heliconia* leaves. Both these nest platforms are very large lanceolate leaves (like those of a large lily), and the nest is attached where the casual observer cannot see it. Hermit nests are long cones made of rootlets and strands of vegetation. They are not lined with down or camouflaged, as are trochilid nests. Instead, they are loosely made, allowing the frequent tropical rains to flow through without saturating either the nest or the eggs. The best way to find a hummingbird nest is to follow the female while she is building it—if she is carrying bits of nesting material, it is likely that she is going to a nest (see photo of a nesting Violet-crowned Hummingbird on color plate A).

Question 11: How does a female hummingbird feed herself while incubating eggs?

Answer: As is the case for most birds, incubating eggs is not a full-time job for the female hummingbird. She must divide her time among taking care of her brood, finding food for herself, and attending to her other needs, such as maintaining her plumage. She may also make unscheduled departures from the nest due to predators or interactions with other animals. William Baltosser, a specialist in the study of nesting, has found that females are quite consistent in the amount of time they spend incubating their eggs, and he suggests that externally induced disruptions may make the difference in whether or not offspring reach maturity (see this chapter, Question 8: How long does it take for hummingbird eggs to hatch?).

The female can normally take a break from time to time to forage for nectar and insects. Even though the temperature of the eggs drops slightly while she is gone, this will not affect their development if the ambient (outside air) temperature is warm. In species like Rufous and Broad-tailed Hummingbirds that nest in colder areas, the egg temperature falls significantly when the female is off the nest, and if she is gone for long periods the development and subsequent hatching of the eggs will be delayed or compromised. If the female cannot feed herself due to bad weather and has to remain on the nest to cover the eggs, she may be forced into a state of torpor. This lowers her body temperature, which in turn lowers the temperature of the incubated eggs and may delay their hatching.

While the young are in the nest, the mother has no problem locating them when she returns from foraging, as she has a vivid visual memory of the nest's location. According to del Hoyo, most young hummingbirds raised in open nests do not make begging calls while they are in the nest, so their vocalizations are not the primary means used by the female to locate the nest. An exception, according to Robert Sargent, a Ruby-throated Hummingbird researcher and bander from Alabama, are the young of this species, which *do* make begging calls from their open nest. Hummingbird young raised in closed nests (spherical nests with an entry hole in the side) begin making calls from the nest four to six days after hatching.

Question 12: How does a female hummingbird feed her nestlings and what do they eat?

Answer: The female gathers nectar for her nestlings to provide energy, and insects to provide them with protein. She stores the gathered supplies in her crop, a saclike enlargement of the esophagus. When she returns to the nest, the young open their bills and point them straight up in the air. The female plunges her bill into a youngster's mouth and down into its crop, where she regurgitates the food (pumps the softened food out of her crop). She feeds them every ten to fifteen minutes when they are very young, with the feeding interval becoming longer as they get older (see also this chapter, Question 13: How quickly do hummingbirds mature?).

The references for Chapter 4, Question 12, include an outstanding video by Don and Noriko Carroll of this feeding process and the entire nesting and reproductive cycle. In the course of extended filming, they observed two unreported behaviors of the female that are of interest for future research. When incubating her eggs, the female reaches down and probes or licks the eggs with her tongue, perhaps to test their temperature or to determine the stage of development of the young by judging the porosity or thickness of the eggs' shells. The Carrolls also noted that when their cat came into the area below the nest, the female appeared to bolt away from the nest. But when they viewed the video in slow motion, it was apparent that the female left the nest and glanced back at it several times before flying away—movements that were not apparent to the naked eye.

William Baltosser studied nest building, incubation, and care of the young in Broad-billed, Violet-crowned, and Black-chinned Hummingbirds, and he found remarkable consistency across species and location in the amount of time they spent at these tasks, especially with regard to incubation. Considered in conjunction with earlier studies, his findings demonstrate "considerable uniformity in nest attentiveness within the Trochilidae."

Question 13: How quickly do hummingbirds mature?

Answer: A hatchling hummingbird weighs less than the egg from which it came. This is because much of the egg material (yolk and albumen) has been broken down into proteins, fats, and carbohydrates to form the developing bird, and waste products that accumulated in the egg have been released as gases and water vapor. When hatched, hummingbirds are naked except for a few downy feathers on the back that are not part of the first juvenile plumage. Their eyes do not open for about five days. When the female comes to feed them, she touches them on the head behind the eye with her bill. This stimulates the young birds to open their mouths (gape) so she can feed them. When the birds are very young, she feeds them several times each hour, reducing the frequency as they get older. Once they are fledged (have left the nest for the first time), she continues feeding them for ten to twenty-five days, until they are completely independent. The number of days the fledglings are fed varies by species and weather conditions. (References for Chapter 4, Question 13, include a video by Rose M. Mayer that shows fledglings taking their first flight.)

Most North American nestlings are ready to fledge approximately twenty days after hatching. The first juvenile feathers begin to come in a few days after hatching. The female broods the hatchlings for ten to twelve days, until they develop enough feathers to regulate their own body temperature. At nineteen or twenty days after hatching, the nestlings sit on the edge of the nest and practice flapping their wings in preparation for flight, and they usually leave the nest at this time or within the next ten days.

A Black-chinned Hummingbird *Archilochus alexandri* nestling that takes twenty days to grow large enough to fledge increases its body weight from less than one-half gram to almost four grams, or 125 percent of the adult's body weight, according to studies on nesting birds in southeastern Arizona by Harold Greeney. The extra weight may be water in the growing feathers. After fledging, the bill continues to grow and the sheathing around the bill hardens. One way to tell if a bird has been recently fledged is to observe whether very fine diagonal corrugations appear along the length of the upper bill. These fine grooves gradually disappear as the bill's external sheath hardens. But you will need the bird in your hand and a ten-power hand lens to see the grooves (see figure 22).

Figure 22. The bill of a juvenile Black-chinned Hummingbird *Archilochus alexandri*. The fine angular corrugations, or grooves, will disappear as the bill hardens.

Question 14: Will young hummingbirds return to a nest after they've left it?

Answer: Most young hummingbirds do not return to their nest once they have fledged (left the nest for the first time), but some may return a few times in the first days after fledging. Once they become independent, they do not return to the nest. Adult females may return to a nest to use it again, or to salvage parts of it for constructing a new nest elsewhere.

FIVE

Flight and Migration

Question 1: How far can a hummingbird fly?

Answer: The distance hummingbirds fly varies from species to species, and even among populations of the same species in different locales (see this chapter, Question 5: Do all hummingbirds migrate?). Some hummingbirds fly very long distances when they migrate, but learning the details about migratory patterns is challenging, since birds must be banded or individually marked and recaptured later in sufficient numbers to yield useful information. Understanding migration is crucial in order to anticipate the consequences of future habitat loss and climate change on bird distribution. Bridget Stutchbury of York University in Toronto and her colleagues attached tiny tracking devices weighing just 0.05 ounces to migratory songbirds to record their movements. When some of the birds were recaptured, the data from their backpacks were downloaded and their daily movements could be mapped. This is a promising development that will be expanded to larger numbers of birds—and perhaps one day greater miniaturization will allow the project to extend to hummingbirds so we can measure exactly how far they fly.

Most hummingbirds found north of Mexico and in southern Argentina and Chile are highly migratory, spending the summer and winter in completely different areas. A bird prepares to migrate by spending a few days to a few weeks feeding and converting sucrose into fat that is stored for the first leg of the journey (see this chapter, Question 2: How are hummingbirds able to fly so far?). As described by William Calder, formerly a University of Arizona ornithologist, the champion migrant is the Rufous Hummingbird. Some banded individuals have traveled a minimum of *2,700 miles one way,* from the northern edge of their nesting range in Alaska to the northern edge of their wintering range in Mexico. This distance equals *49 million* body lengths, one of the longest migrations in proportion to size of any creature. The trip is not accomplished all in one flight, but rather in a series of short flights from one flower patch or feeding area to the next.

Robert Gill and colleagues from the Alaska Science Center used satellite telemetry and surgically implanted transmitters to track shorebirds, Bar-tailed Godwits *Limosa lapponica baueri,* that migrate nonstop across the central Pacific Ocean, a distance of almost 4,500 miles. Scientists have considered oceans, mountain ranges, ice fields, and deserts as barriers to the movement of land-dependent animals, but this research suggests that a trans-oceanic route may function as "an ecological corridor rather than a barrier, providing a wind-assisted passage relatively free of pathogens and predators." The research has fascinating implications for understanding how Ruby-throated Hummingbirds manage their migration across the Gulf of Mexico, a distance of about five hundred miles, and the longest nonstop migration route of any species of hummingbird. In proportion to the relative distances and sizes of the birds, it surpasses the achievement of the Bar-tailed Godwits, approximately one hundred times larger, crossing the Pacific Ocean.

If hummingbirds fly over the water at their normal speed of about twenty-five miles per hour, it would take them twenty hours to make the trip. We assume that this flight starts when the weather is good, often in late afternoon, and continues overnight so that birds reach land in early morning daylight. We expect that birds once underway fly with the most advantageous winds that will carry them in the right direction, increasing their speed and shortening the time needed to cross the water. Birds can move up and down to fly at different altitudes, taking

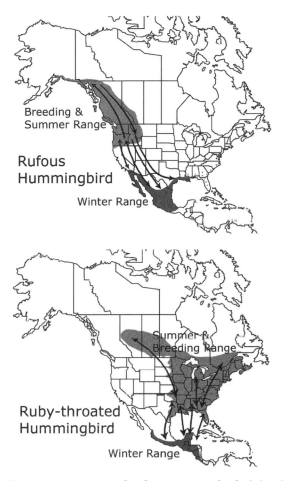

Figure 23. *Top*, migration routes of Rufous Hummingbirds *Selasphorus rufus*, from their northern breeding range that extends to just south of Anchorage, Alaska, to Mexico and the Gulf Coast of the United States. Researchers believe that most of the population travels a circular route, flying north along the Pacific Coast from Mexico through California to their breeding grounds in the north, and returning south along the Rocky Mountain chain; *bottom*, migration routes of Ruby-throated Hummingbirds *Archilochus colubris* to their wintering range in Mexico and Central America. Some individuals winter in the southern tip of Florida.

advantage of favorable winds to help their migration travel. Tara Rodden Robinson, an ornithologist from the University of Illinois, reported that not all Ruby-throats cross the water, and many move south along the Texas and Mexico coast or overland in Mexico (see figure 23).

Question 2: How are hummingbirds able to fly so far?

Answer: Hummingbirds, like most long-distance migratory birds, are able to accumulate large amounts of body fat that serve as stored-up energy for migration. Before a migratory flight, hummingbirds consume more than their usual daily requirement of nectar, converting the extra sugars to glycogen that is stored in the liver. The liver then converts the glycogen to fat that is stored throughout the body. It may take several days to get enough nectar from flowers to accumulate the necessary energy resources for one leg of the trip.

Although you might think a hummingbird could just drink from your feeder as much as it needed all at once for the trip, the conversion and storage process takes time. Sugar is consumed, held temporarily in the crop, digested, and stored as glycogen in the liver. The stored glycogen is converted into glucose and then burned within minutes or hours of its consumption, so there must be an oversupply before the glycogen is converted to fat and stored. Sugar contains only four calories per gram, while fat contains nine calories per gram, and fat is a more stable compound that can be stored in lipid cells throughout the body for long periods of time. The primary storage areas are in the neck region (above the clavicle or wishbone), in the belly (all around the internal organs below the breastbone), and along the bird's back. A hummingbird can store up to half its total body weight as fat in preparation for a long migratory flight.

Hummingbirds are a relatively ancient group of birds that evolved long before songbirds (passerines), and therefore research findings on the migratory behavior of other birds such as warblers, thrushes, and sparrows may not apply to hummingbirds. The discussion in this and the next question explains what might be happening in hummingbirds, but it may not be completely accurate. This is another area for future research.

An interdisciplinary research team led by Niels Rattenborg at the University of Wisconsin–Madison studied how Gambel's White-crowned Sparrows *Zonotrichia leucophrys gambelii* prepare for migration. They found that these normally diurnal birds make their long-distance migrations at night, as may be true of some hummingbirds, and that when in a migratory state, the sparrows spent about two-thirds less time sleeping than was normal for them between migratory periods. The researchers tested the cognitive functioning of the birds during the period when they were getting less sleep and found that they performed quite well; in contrast, their cognitive functioning declined measurably after only one night of experimenter-induced sleep deprivation during a nonmigratory period. The researchers concluded that "despite their apparent sleep loss, migrating songbirds are capable of engaging in adaptive waking behaviors including prolonged flight, navigation, foraging, and evading predators in novel environments." Would similar results be obtained if hummingbirds were the subjects of the research?

An important piece of research on Swainson's Thrush *Catharus ustulatus* also might have implications for understanding hummingbird migratory behavior. Caged thrushes exhibit nocturnal sleeplessness and restless behavior during the times of year when they would be migrating if they were in the wild. Behavioral neuroscientist Verner Bingman, eco-physiologist Frank Moore, and graduate student Thomas Fuchs observed caged thrushes for a year, keeping records of when and how long they slept. During the fall and spring when this species is normally migrating, they stayed awake at night and did several interesting things during the day that apparently compensated for the lack of sleep. They took very short naps, averaging just nine seconds at a time. They also engaged in another form of sleep, unilateral eye closure, closing one eye and resting one half of their brain while the other eye and brain hemisphere remained alert. They also spent time in a drowsy state, fluffing their feathers and partly shutting both eyes while remaining somewhat alert.

These types of sleep postures are not typical of diurnal birds during the nonmigratory period, when birds spend only 2 or 3 percent of their time sleeping during the day, according to the researchers. They suggest that these naps and resting periods compensate for sleep deprivation and still allow the bird to forage and replenish its energy supplies during the day. It will be interesting to see if these findings apply in any way to hummingbird behavior.

Question 3: What tells a hummingbird when to migrate?

Answer: Circadian rhythms are part of life for most organisms, coordinating our activities with the day/night cycle. When we travel between time zones or do not get enough sleep, most of us feel somewhat out of sorts. A great deal of research creating artificial light/dark situations in laboratories has demonstrated that the behavior of virtually all animals studied is sensitive to circadian rhythms. Circannual rhythms (from *circa* meaning "around," and *annus* meaning "year") are similar to circadian rhythms, but they are related to seasonal migratory behavior, triggered by both internal impulses and seasonal factors like the length of the day, changes in temperature and humidity, and the availability of food.

Hummingbirds evolved in the tropics, where there was no need for migration, but many species have dispersed and now live part of their lives in areas where the seasons change, and so they need to migrate to survive. The increasing hours of daylight (photoperiod) are the cue for songbirds to begin preparing for migration, but this may not be the stimulus for hummingbirds. For example, Anna's and Costa's Hummingbirds move north in winter and begin breeding in December, before the photoperiod has begun to increase. Many hummingbird species are permanent residents, especially those living near the equator, and although they may not respond to day-length changes, there must be other cues that stimulate them to begin their breeding season.

The instinct to migrate is so well ingrained in the humming-birds that summer in North America that you do not have to worry that the presence of feeders in your yard will entice the birds to remain there instead of migrating. Hummingbirds will visit your feeders in late summer and fall, get fat, and then depart on schedule, despite the surplus nectar easily available in your feeder.

Question 4: How do hummingbirds find their way during migration?

Answer: Almost all migratory birds studied have shown the ability to navigate by the position of the sun during the day and the position of the stars at night. They have an internal clock that tells them in what compass direction the sun should be during the day and where the constellations should be at night. No studies have been conducted on hummingbirds, and we can only postulate that they respond to the same cues as other birds. They do have an amazing visual memory (see Chapter 2, Question 1: Are hummingbirds intelligent?), and we can assume at least that when the hummingbird nears its destination, it uses its visual memory to pinpoint its exact location. A question remains regarding how juvenile birds, which have never made the journey before, are able to find their way alone to their final destination on their wintering grounds.

Just as the needle of a handheld compass points to magnetic north, many birds have a sort of magnetic compass that orients them to the earth's magnetic field. They can calculate instinctively the direction in which they need to fly to reach their destination. Dominik Heyers and his colleagues at the University of California, Irvine, studied how a bird can intuit the earth's magnetic field through brief chemical impulses in the retina that indicate when the bird is facing magnetic north. Again, we know of no research that tells us if hummingbirds possess such a magnetic compass.

Question 5: Do all hummingbirds migrate?

Answer: The mild winter weather along the Pacific Coast and in lowland tropical forests offers a suitable year-round home for local hummingbirds, and so these birds have no need to migrate. Most tropical hummingbirds seem to be nomadic, moving from one nectar-rich area to another without a need to travel far, since there are usually no cold temperatures and few food shortages to avoid. Some populations in the tropics move from high on the mountains to the lowlands when storms or unseasonable cold force them to find a better climate with more nectar sources, but again, they have no need to migrate.

John Rappole of the Smithsonian National Zoo and Karl Schuchmann of the Alexander Koenig Museum in Bonn, Germany, analyzed the available data on hummingbird movement and migration. They found that forty-nine species, mostly in subtropical and tropical regions, were classified as wanderers or dispersers. Birds in this group move only a few kilometers from where they nested to search for a better food supply or in response to being chased away by more dominant birds, and they could either return to their breeding area or establish new residence elsewhere. A larger group of eighty-seven hummingbird species of subtropical and tropical regions made altitudinal movements, moving up and down mountains with the seasons, depending on food supply and climate. Forty-two species made short latitudinal movements (ten to one thousand kilometers), returning to their breeding areas each year. Finally, twenty-nine species made long-distance latitudinal migrations of more than one thousand kilometers between established breeding and wintering areas each year. This migrating group was further divided into thirteen species that migrate from northern regions to subtropical regions, fifteen species that moved from southern temperate regions to the subtropics and tropics, and one species that is known to move from Panama across the equator to southern Brazil and points between and return the following year. This broad spectrum of migration movements reveals that hummingbirds have evolved many different methods of contending

Ruby-throated Hummingbird *Archilochus colubris*. Bombay Hook National Wildlife Refuge, Delaware. The most common hummingbird east of the Mississippi River. *Photograph by George C. West*

Violet-crowned Hummingbird *Amazilia violiceps*. Patagonia, Arizona. A Mexican hummingbird established in the United States only in southeastern Arizona. *Photograph by George C. West*

Anna's Hummingbird *Calypte anna*. Green Valley, Arizona. A common hummingbird along the Pacific coast and southern Arizona. The brilliant rose red of males also appears gold or black depending on the light angle. *Photograph courtesy of Allen J. Tozier*

Violet-crowned Hummingbird *Amazilia violiceps* on its nest near Patagonia, Arizona. Note the lichens that camouflage the nest in a sycamore tree. *Photograph courtesy of Jim Burns*

Calliope Hummingbird *Stellula calliope*. Phoenix, Arizona. The smallest hummingbird in the United States, common from southern British Columbia south to California. *Photograph courtesy of Jim Burns*

Rufous Hummingbird *Selasphorus rufus*. Greer, Arizona. Common migrant in fall in the Rocky Mountains from Colorado south through Arizona and New Mexico. *Photograph courtesy of Allen J. Tozier*

Broad-tailed Hummingbird *Selasphorus platycercus*. Greer, Arizona. Abundant breeder throughout the Rocky Mountain high-elevation forests. *Photograph courtesy of Allen J. Tozier*

Plain-capped Starthroat *Heliomaster constantii*. Patagonia, Arizona. A rare visitor to southern Arizona from Mexico. *Photograph courtesy of Allen J. Tozier*

C

Broad-billed Hummingbird *Cynanthus latirostris*. Patagonia, Arizona. A Mexican hummingbird that nests commonly in southern Arizona. *Photograph by George C. West*

Berylline Hummingbird *Amazilia beryllina*. Madera Canyon, Arizona. A Mexican species that is an annual visitor and rare breeder in Arizona. *Photograph courtesy of Jim Burns*

Tufted Coquette *Lophornis ornatus*. Trinidad. *Photograph courtesy of David J. Southall*

Crimson Topaz *Topaza pella*. Bolivar State, Venezuela. *Photograph courtesy of David J. Southall*

Lucifer Hummingbird *Calothrorax lucifer.* Ash Canyon, Arizona. A Mexican dry brush species found in the United States only in southeastern Arizona and the Big Bend area of south Texas.

Costa's Hummingbird *Calypte costae.* Green Valley, Arizona. A bird of the California, Arizona, and Baja California deserts.

White-eared Hummingbird *Hylocharis leucotis.* Madera Canyon, Arizona. A common hummingbird in the Sierra Madre of Mexico, found annually in southeastern Arizona, southern New Mexico, and Texas.

Buff-bellied Hummingbird *Amazilia yucatanensis.* Naples, Florida. Common in the Gulf Coast of Mexico and southeastern Texas.

Magnificent Hummingbird *Eugenes fulgens.* Madera Canyon, Arizona. Montane hummingbird common throughout Mexico and well established in southeastern Arizona.

Rufous Hummingbird *Selasphorus rufus.* Homer, Alaska. Nests farther north than any other hummingbird, and migrates to Mexico.

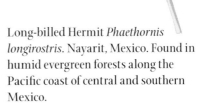

Azure-crowned Hummingbird *Amazilia cyanocephala*. Oaxaca, Mexico. Pine-oak and evergreen forests of southern Mexico.

Long-billed Hermit *Phaethornis longirostris*. Nayarit, Mexico. Found in humid evergreen forests along the Pacific coast of central and southern Mexico.

Amethyst-throated Hummingbird *Lampornis amethystinus*. Nayarit, Mexico. A large hummingbird of the humid forests of central and southern Mexico.

Blue-throated Hummingbird *Lampornis clemenciae*. Madera Canyon, Arizona. Resident of pine-oak and evergreen mountain woodlands of northern Mexico and the sky islands of Arizona, New Mexico, into Texas.

Booted Racket-tail *Ocreatus underwoodii*. South America. *Illustration by George C. West from a video frame by Tom Kaminski*

Chestnut-breasted Coronet *Boisson-neaua matthewsii*. Tandayapa Valley, Ecuador. *Photograph courtesy of Bill Maynard*

Collared Inca *Coeligena torquata*. Cabanas San Isidro, Ecuador. *Photograph courtesy of Bill Maynard*

Tawny-bellied Hermit *Phaethornis syrmatophorus*. Tandayapa Valley, Ecuador. *Photograph courtesy of Bill Maynard*

Saw-billed Hermit *Rhamphodon naevius*. Ubatuba, São Paulo, Brazil. *Photograph courtesy of Arthur Grosset*

Fork-tailed Woodnymph *Thalurania furcata*. Brazil, east of the Andes. *Photograph courtesy of Arthur Grosset*

Juan Fernandez Firecrown *Sephanoides fernandensis*. Robinson Crusoe Island, Chile. *Photograph courtesy of Arthur Grosset*

Bearded Helmetcrest *Oxypogon guerinii*. Merida State, Venezuela. *Photograph courtesy of David J. Southall*

Sombre Hummingbird *Campylopterus cirrochloris*. Ubatuba, São Paulo, Brazil. *Photograph courtesy of Arthur Grosset*

Orange-throated Sunangel *Heliangelus mavors*. Merida State, Venezuela. *Photograph courtesy of David J. Southall*

Swallow-tailed Hummingbird *Eupetomena macrourus*. São Paulo, Brazil. *Photograph courtesy of Arthur Grosset*

Black Jacobin *Florisuga fuscus*. Ubatuba, São Paulo, Brazil. *Photograph courtesy of Arthur Grosset*

with limited food supplies and habitat for nesting and wintering (see also Chapter 1, Question 3: Where in the world are hummingbirds found?).

Not all North American species of hummingbirds follow the same migration schedule. While most fly north in spring, breed in summer, and return south in fall, some Anna's and Costa's Hummingbirds that nest in Arizona and as far north as Washington state start their southward trip in September and October. They winter in Mexico for a few months and return to the California coast (Anna's) or desert (Costa's) to nest from December through February. In contrast, Rufous Hummingbirds that nest from northern Oregon to southern Alaska do not arrive on their nesting grounds until March in Oregon and late April to late May in Alaska. Their time in the north is very short and they return southward starting in July and August and begin to arrive in Mexico in September and October, reaching their greatest numbers there in December.

In general, adult males migrate both north and south before females do. In fall, males leave when their reproductive duties are over; females follow when the young are fledged and have wandered away from the nesting area. The young usually migrate at the same time or later than the females. South American species that breed in far southern regions probably migrate north to more temperate areas to spend the austral winter (referring to winter in the southern hemisphere, as contrasted with the boreal or northern winter). We do not know of any published information on the timing, extent, or routes of this movement, so this is a wide-open area for future research.

Most populations of North American hummingbirds that do migrate end up in Mexico, although a few go only as far as the south coastal United States. The exact ranges of wintering hummingbirds are still being studied in Mexico. Jonathan Moran, ornithologist from Royal Roads University in Vancouver, British Columbia, is using deuterium (^{2}H), a stable isotope of hydrogen that is stored in the feathers of Rufous Hummingbirds, to locate the latitude of their wintering range in Mexico. Deuterium from precipitation is taken up by plants and is present in nectar.

When hummingbirds consume nectar, deuterium is stored in the feathers that form during the annual molt. The amount of deuterium stored in the feathers, known as the "deuterium signature," is directly related to the latitude where the feather was formed.

In the United States, many biologists are actively banding hummingbirds in winter, especially in the Gulf of Mexico states and on the Atlantic coast where an increasing number of western hummingbirds are overwintering. For some reason, perhaps global warming, Rufous Hummingbirds are becoming more common in the southern and eastern coastal United States in winter. About once a week, we hear that someone in Maryland or Pennsylvania has banded an Allen's or Rufous Hummingbird, and there are many reports of repeat visitors to feeding and banding stations in the Southeast. Some individuals may have learned that flying to the warmth of Alabama is easier than going all the way to central Mexico, and eventually we will discover their migration routes through banding (see Chapter 9, Question 5: Why do researchers band hummingbirds?).

A falsehood that has been repeated many times is that hummingbirds migrate south on the backs of geese. There is no evidence to support this claim—it is simply not true. Hummingbirds make their migratory journeys on their own. Most hummingbirds that leave North America in the fall depart before geese are ready to begin their own migration, and almost all species of geese that migrate from Canada and the northern United States go only as far as the southern states and not into central Mexico, where most North American hummingbirds winter. If you were a hummingbird, a goose would be a bad choice for transportation because it would be late departing, and it would not take you all the way to your destination.

SIX

Dangers and Defenses

Question 1: What are the natural predators of hummingbirds?

Answer: For a human, a bite of hummingbird would not be very satisfying. But for some animals, a nice hummingbird, loaded with nectar and perhaps stuffed with fat before its migration, makes a hardy and nutritious meal. Although hummingbirds are tiny, most weighing only a few grams (a fraction of an ounce), they have many natural and some unwelcome, unnatural predators. The most efficient hummingbird predator is probably the domestic or feral cat. Yes, letting your sweet little fluffy pussycat outside into the garden may spell the end for several of your favorite hummingbirds. Eggs and young hummingbirds are also routinely consumed by small mammals, including some bats, as well as by predatory birds like jays, crows, ravens, and toucans.

In anthropomorphic terms, hummingbirds can seem arrogant. They often appear to feel supremely sure that they are faster and more skillful at dodging a predator than is any other bird, and it is not unusual for them to seemingly ignore the potential for predation while they are intent on their nectar-feeding activities. Cats, snakes, large lizards, roadrunners (birds), and even praying mantises take advantage of this attitude by remaining immobile, waiting for an unwary bird to get just close enough to snatch. Hummingbird feeders hung from the eaves of a house or too near a tree or bush will entice these predators to climb up on a window ledge or tree branch and wait for birds to hover at the feeder within easy reach.

With their rapid, blurry wing motion, small hummingbirds are sometimes taken for insects and preyed upon by animals that don't normally eat birds. Two insects that apparently make this mistake are praying mantises and dragonflies, and there are said to be records of frogs and even of a bass capturing hummingbirds, almost certainly because they were perceived as insects.

Other predators do not lie in wait. Small raptors like the American Kestrel, Merlin, and Sharp-shinned Hawk capture perching hummingbirds when they rest in a bush with their eyes shut, as they typically do during midday. Some hawks and some of the larger members of the flycatcher family are even able to catch the birds in flight. Brilliantly colored members of the tanager family have been seen catching and eating hummingbirds, and small owls can find sleeping hummingbirds at night. Hummingbirds sometimes get caught in spider webs as they collect bits of the webbing to glue their nesting materials together. Birds have to be wary of a large and sticky web and of the spider that maintains it.

Insects that bite and sting such as ants, bees, and wasps usually do not pose a danger to hummingbirds, although these insects may share some of the same nectar sources. Hummingbirds usually bypass flowers that are filled with ants or honey bees, or those at which a large solitary wasp is at work.

Question 2: How do hummingbirds defend themselves and their food supply?

Answer: Their primary defense is their ability to escape through rapid reaction and flight, and they have excellent eyesight that helps them see potential danger (see Chapter 2, Question 15: Do hummingbirds have good eyesight?). If a predator grabs at a hummingbird from behind, its loosely attached tail feathers easily pull out, giving the bird a chance to escape (the feathers grow back quickly). Hummingbirds do not have any physical defenses except against their own kind. There are examples of hummingbirds being impaled by another hummingbird's bill and both eventually perishing. The birds use their feet when fighting with each other—the feet, although relatively small, have claws of long and sharp curved toenails that can do some damage to another hummingbird (see figure 19).

Some hummingbirds defend their nectar sources by claiming sole control of a feeder, challenging any other hummingbird that approaches it, regardless of size, species, sex, or age. Continued territorial defense of a feeder or flower patch can require the expenditure of a great deal of energy, and if an overwhelming number of challengers appear, the bird will give up.

Hummingbirds may attempt to drive away raptors and other large birds that are potential predators, usually by repeated rapid diving at and buzzing of the intruder, rather than by physical contact (see figure 18 illustrating a dive display). In some cases, hummingbirds join together (or with other bird species) to chase away predators. Female hummingbirds attack anything they view as a threat to the nest or nestlings, including humans.

Harold Greeney and Susan Wethington have found that Black-chinned Hummingbirds *Archilochus alexandri* in southeastern Arizona may have greater success in raising their young to the fledging stage if they build their nest in the vicinity of a raptor (Cooper's Hawk or Goshawk) nest. The presence of the hawk may discourage other predatory birds and small mammals from raiding the hummingbird's nest and eating the eggs or young. This prevention of nest predation by capitalizing on the superior defense abilities of other species occurs widely in the avian world.

Question 3: Do hummingbirds get sick?

Answer: Certainly hummingbirds can get sick, and if an illness in a wild bird diminishes its ability to fly and eat, it will die within a few hours. Constant access to a source of nutrition is critical to a hummingbird's survival, so anything that prevents or interferes with its ability to find food results in death, and the most common problems in hummingbirds are due to insufficient caloric intake and lack of protein. This can be the consequence of poor conditions in the habitat or of disability due to an illness or injury to the wing or other body part that prevents foraging.

Holly Ernest, a research veterinarian from the University of California, Davis, points out that just like people and our pets, hummingbirds occasionally show evidence of diseases or abnormalities. They are vulnerable to the full spectrum of pathogens and parasites that affect humans and other animals—viruses, bacteria, protozoan parasites, worm parasites, and fungi—although little is known about how these disease organisms specifically affect hummingbirds. One of the more common diseases seen in some areas is a wartlike growth on the legs or head that may be caused by a virus. The avian (bird) poxvirus causes these growths, which can lead to the loss of a foot and result in an inability to feed. Other viruses, bacteria, and injuries can cause growths that look similar to those caused by avian pox. Hummingbirds are also susceptible to West Nile virus infections. Since hummingbirds, like all wildlife, as well as humans, can carry germs that infect other species, wash your hands and use safe handling practices to prevent germs from being transmitted from hummingbird feeders to you (see also Chapter 7 for a discussion of sanitary practices with hummingbird feeders).

Pathologist Andre Saidenberg and his colleagues working in Sao Paolo, Brazil, reported on a Swallow-tailed Hummingbird *Eupetomena macroura* that was brought to the Sorocaba Zoo by local birdwatchers. They had found the bird prostrate on the ground and unable to fly. The bird died after two days in their hospital, and it was found to have been infected with *Serratia marcesens,* not a normal component of the microflora of the hummingbird digestive tract. This is an enterobacterium, a type of bacteria that can cause serious infections in humans, including meningitis, conjunctivitis, and cystitis, and various diseases in other animals. The researchers could not ascertain the cause of the infection, but since it seemed to originate in the digestive tract, they speculated that a contaminated feeder could have been involved. In their article they mention that fungal diseases such as candidiasis and aspergillosis are common in captive hummingbirds (this is echoed in the Husbandry Guidelines for Hummingbirds from the European Association of Zoos and Aquaria), and that other diseases such as salmonellosis and mycobacteriosis have been documented.

Clearly, hummingbirds maintained in aviaries and at feeders may contract fungal diseases as a consequence of poor sanitation or bad food, and they are particularly vulnerable if they are immune suppressed due to stressful conditions that can result from overcrowding. Even honey used in a feeder can lead to candidiasis, a fungus of the palate, which may be indicated by a bird's keeping the tip of its tongue outside its bill. This is one of the few treatable illnesses in hummingbirds. Nystatin, an antifungal drug, produces good results in just a few days, as reported by biologist Karen Krebbs of the Arizona-Sonora Desert Museum (see also Chapter 7, Question 5: How do I make nectar to put in my hummingbird feeder?).

Jack Roovers, a successful private hummingbird breeder in the Netherlands and a source of information for the EAZA Husbandry Guidelines for Hummingbirds, shared with us his treatment for the fungal disease aspergillosis. Roovers uses dissolvable Sporonax and Triporal capsules to treat the illness. Neither medication can simply be dissolved in a sugar solution and accepted by the birds, but he has developed a detailed procedure that results in a mixture that is acceptable to the birds and treats the fungus successfully. The course of treatment he uses is to add two drops of the mixture to thirty milliliters of nectar preparation each day, and to feed it to the affected bird for ten days. Even if an oral medication can be administered to a hummingbird in the nectar, it is difficult to ensure delivery of the correct dosage because a bird that is ill may have a poor appetite. We include this material to highlight the personal and specialized nature of the state of the art of medical treatment for captive hummingbirds, but we caution the reader not to use medicines without proper training and veterinary advice, and not to try to medicate wild birds (see also Chapter 8, Question 6: Why are there so few hummingbird exhibits in zoos and museums?).

Question 4: Do hummingbirds get parasites?

Answer: Hummingbirds, like most wild vertebrates, are susceptible to external and internal parasites. They may be bitten by blood-sucking insects like hippoboscid flies (flat flies that fit between the feathers of birds), feather lice and mites, and nasal mites that spend their entire life cycle inside the nasal passages of birds (see figure 24). Most of these external parasites are found by people such as bird banders who handle the live birds, or they are discovered on a bird that recently died. There is no evidence that feather lice or mite infestations have actually killed a hummingbird. As with other species of birds and other animals, hummingbirds can harbor harmful parasites inside their blood cells. One of these blood parasites, *Haemoproteus archilochus*, was identified in the Ruby-throated Hummingbird by Gediminas Valkiunas of Lithuania and an international group studying blood parasites of birds in northwestern Costa Rica.

It is not uncommon for coccidia (a protozoan intestinal parasite) and tapeworms to be found in the small intestine of birds that eat arthropods. Hummingbirds can survive for many years with these parasites in their intestine, and they may only be

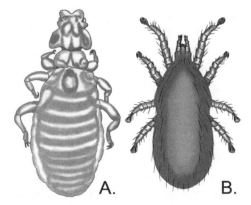

Figure 24. Hummingbird parasites: *A:* hummingbird louse. (*Illustration based on a photograph by Ummat Somjee, Grouse Mountain Refuge for Endangered Wildlife, North Vancouver, B.C., Canada.*); *B,* hummingbird nasal mite.

A.   B.

found on necropsy when the bird dies. Holly Ernest notes that hummingbirds have occasionally been reported sick and dying from other parasitic diseases of the intestinal tract such as *microsporidiosis* and *encephalitozoon*.

Question 5: How are flower mites dependent on hummingbirds?

Answer: Flower mites are a group of tiny arachnids (spider family) one-half to one millimeter or less than one-sixteenth of an inch long. Of the many species of flower mites, most are concentrated in the tropics, where they are fairly specialized, living in the flowers of only one species or a group of related species of flowers. The mites are so numerous and so hungry that they drink up to half the nectar a flower can produce each day, often sharing nectar sources with hummingbirds.

Not satisfied with drinking half the nectar, flower mites use hummingbirds for transportation to other flowers. The mites have no eyes, but they can smell and sense when a hummingbird probes a flower. Being careful that the hummingbird does not grab them as a protein snack, several mites can run across the flower and jump onto the hummingbird's bill in a matter of seconds, run up the bill, and hide in the bird's nostrils. As the hummingbird moves from flower to flower, the mite can smell when the hummingbird is at its host flower and it simply jumps off. This constant movement of mites from flower to flower insures survival of the mites by providing access to a wide range of mating partners but does little for the hummingbird. While in the bird's nostrils, the mites do not take anything from the hummingbird, according to Robert Colwell, evolutionary biologist from the University of Connecticut, so we cannot consider them parasites.

Question 6: What dangers do hummingbirds face in the environment?

Answer: Apart from predators, weather and lack of food are the two most critical dangers hummingbirds face. Because of their small size, they must eat almost constantly to maintain their body temperature, and if the weather is stormy enough to prevent them from flying, they are unable to search for food (see Chapter 2, Question 3: Why do hummingbirds need to eat so much?). Without enough to eat, they lower their body temperature and wait, hoping that when they rouse from torpor they will find the needed nectar. If not, they will die (see Chapter 2, Question 11: How do hummingbirds conserve energy?). When flower nectar is scarce, hummingbirds have been seen to lick up the honeydew excrement of coccids, scale insects that excrete fluid with a high sugar content. Hummingbirds can survive below-freezing temperatures with snow on the ground as long as there are insects flying, sap running in the trees, a few flowers with nectar in bloom, or a friendly hummingbird feeder hanging in a backyard.

It is helpful to provide a hummingbird feeder in cold weather, but it is energetically costly for the birds to take in large volumes of cold nectar. They need to warm the nectar to body temperature so they can properly digest it, and this requires them to increase their metabolic rate. Chris Lotz and Carlos Martinez del Rio of the University of Wyoming, along with S. W. Nicholson of the University of Pretoria, South Africa, created a mathematical formula to predict the amount of energy used in warming nectar, based on experiments in which they compared the metabolism of Rufous Hummingbirds fed nectar at body temperature (thirty-nine degrees Celsius) with the same birds fed nectar at four degrees Celsius. Hummingbirds feeding on the cold solution have to increase their metabolic rate, according to these researchers, as much as if the ambient temperature dropped by fifteen degrees Celsius. This is an important aspect of understanding the energy consumption of birds in various climates.

Loss of habitat is another factor that reduces hummingbird populations. This includes forests and brush land cleared for grazing and mining, land used for the deposition of mining waste, land cleared by wildfires or human-set fires, land used for roads (the roadway itself and the fragmentation of habitat that building a road causes), and land lost to urbanization. Douglas Bolger, Thomas Scott, and John Rotenberry, working in San Diego County, California, showed that while some birds including Anna's Hummingbird *Calypte anna* increase their populations as land is developed for housing, others such as Costa's Hummingbirds *Calypte costae* do not. Habitat can also be lost through the introduction of nonnative species such as domestic cats, cattle and other grazing animals, rats, mice, and their predators such as mongoose. The use of herbicides and pesticides and the introduction of nonnative vegetation like most grain crops and buffelgrass or African foxtail *Cenchrus ciliaris* (a problem in Arizona) can also cause habitat to disappear.

Perhaps the most serious current threat to hummingbirds is climate change. With the warming climate, the cycles of their nectar plants along with the amount and timing of nectar availability are changing. If the decrease in nectar availability becomes severe enough, migrating hummingbirds may not be able to find the needed resources to reach their breeding grounds. It is not known if hummingbirds will be able to adjust the timing of their movement patterns to changes in nectar availability from their normal plant resources.

Question 7: What dangers do hummingbirds face from people?

Answer: People frequently cause injury and death to hummingbirds. Any windows that reflect the trees and plants outside can be dangerous to all birds, including hummingbirds, and windows that are situated where an approaching bird can see through the house and through a window on the opposite wall are especially dangerous, as the bird may perceive them as an outdoor shortcut. Although not very attractive, strips of ribbon or string hung from the top of the window frame can make birds more cautious when approaching the glass. Hummingbirds are more curious than other birds, and the presence of moving ribbons or the light bouncing off an old CD hanging in the window may alert them to a potential hazard.

With their incredible ability to maneuver in flight, hummingbirds have a greater chance of avoiding a collision than do larger birds. Birds that hit windows at high speed are unlikely to survive, but some only knock themselves out temporarily and recover. If a bird flies into your window and falls to the ground, it is best to carefully pick the bird up to keep it from being caught by a predator. Just place it high in a secure spot outdoors until it recovers and flies away. Trying to rehabilitate an injured bird, especially a hummingbird, should be left to the experts (see Chapter 9, Question 7: What should I do if I see or rescue an injured hummingbird?).

Question 8: How can I get a hummingbird safely out of my house if it has accidentally entered?

Answer: Open windows and doors in any structure can be death traps for hummingbirds, because once a bird wanders or is enticed inside, it is likely to fly to the ceiling in its attempt to escape. It does not understand the concept of a ceiling, since in nature and in birds' experience there is always a way up and around overhanging leaves and branches. They do not seem to understand that the daylight they see through an open window or door is the way out.

There are several ways to get a hummingbird out of a building. The first is to make the inside of the building as dark as possible, so the bird cannot see. (If you open a door or window, usually the light seeping into the room will cause the bird to go up to the ceiling.) In a dark room, you can find the bird by using a flashlight, as it may drop to a place within easy reach. Then you can catch the bird and release it outside. If you have a long-handled insect or butterfly net (soft fabric of small mesh, not a coarse fishing net) and a flashlight to help you locate the bird, you can sometimes scoop the bird in the net, hold the bag of the net closed, and release the bird outside.

If you cannot darken the building or room, the bird will continue to bump against the ceiling or perch high out of reach, and chasing it around will only tire you both out. In this situa-

Figure 25. Feeder on the end of a long pole, used to coax a hummingbird from inside a building.

tion, if you have a hummingbird feeder that the bird may have used outside, raise the feeder slowly (on the end of a pole if possible) toward the bird (see figure 25). Since the bird has to feed very frequently when it is active, it should not be long before the bird is hungry and will be tempted to land on the feeder. Slowly lower the feeder or move the pole so that the feeder is close to an open door or even out the door, and the bird will escape (see also Chapter 9, Question 7: What should I do if I see or rescue an injured hummingbird?).

SEVEN

Attracting and Feeding

Question 1: Are hummingbirds friendly?

Answer: Hummingbirds are curious and may approach you when you are wearing bright-colored clothing, especially if the clothing is red or orange. They may even probe at you, believing that the clothing might be flowers and a source of nectar. But they are not being "friendly," which is a human term. When a wild animal approaches, it is usually exploring to see if you represent danger, food, or a potential mate—not to be confused with a domesticated animal that may approach to be petted. Hummingbirds assume that any intruder, including you, is a potential competitor or threat, and their instinct is to defend their territory or food reserves. This is an issue of survival for them, because immediate access to food is critical due to their high metabolism.

Some hummingbird species are more tolerant than others of humans, according to Claudia Rodriguez-Flores, hummingbird biologist from Iztacala, Mexico. She notes that Berylline Hummingbirds *Amazilia beryllina* are very timid, but Broad-billed *Cyanthus latirostris* and *Selasphorus* hummingbirds, Broad-tailed, Rufous, and Allen's appear much more confident around humans (personal communication).

Question 2: How can I attract hummingbirds to my garden or feeder?

Answer: Hummingbirds are attracted to your garden by the plants that they can feed from or hide in. They also may come to drink or bathe in clean water you have set out for them. In Appendix A we list some books that describe in detail the plants that hummingbirds prefer in specific parts of the United States and Canada, and we have included an abbreviated list in Appendix A to get you started. If you have limited outdoor space or live where there is little vegetation, your best bet is to grow a few potted plants or shrubs that appeal to hummingbirds and hang one or two feeders in your yard or from your window.

A water feature, even a small shallow birdbath, will entice hummingbirds to stop by. Make sure that if you have a water feature with a fast-flowing waterfall, you also have an area where water flows more gently over a flat surface. The depth of the water should be one-quarter of an inch or less. A slow drip or water mist that collects on a flat surface or shallow pan will also attract hummingbirds to drink or bathe. Hummingbirds like to bathe one or more times each day and will flutter in the water, then perch nearby to shake their wings and feathers to remove excess water and to preen. In the wild, they find natural areas in which to bathe, including water flowing over rocks, large leaves that fill with water in a rain, or dew on plants or grass in the early morning. Hummingbirds have been observed diving into a pool of water, submerging, then popping to the surface and flying off.

In eastern North America, you may have seen only Ruby-throated Hummingbirds at your feeder, but western and southern species have been occurring in the east with increasing frequency. Some of the rarer hummingbirds are traveling farther north and arriving later in the fall than expected. Where there are artificial feeders, they seem to be remaining longer in areas in which they would normally perish due to the cold and lack of nutrition. We recommend that you keep feeders up for a week or more after the last hummingbird has departed in the fall, just in case there are stragglers. Once freezing weather has settled in, take your feeder down until spring unless you know or suspect that there is a vagrant hummingbird in the area. In southern areas, consider leaving your feeder up all year, as there is a greater likelihood of attracting one of the rare visitors to your area. If you find a rarity, let your local birding hotline or Audubon Society know about it. That way, others can see it, or an expert can make a positive identification that often includes trapping and banding the bird so its movements can be tracked.

Question 3: Will hummingbirds feed only from red flowers?

Answer: Because many of the long tubular flowers hummingbirds prefer are red or shades of orange or pink, people tend to think that hummingbirds are attracted only to these hues. In reality, hummingbirds will feed from any flower that has a good supply of nectar. Hummingbird feeder manufacturers believe in the power of red as well, as evidenced by the fact that almost all artificial feeders are partly or entirely red. Some feeders have a yellow insert at the feeder port, but yellow is more attractive to bees than to hummingbirds and it is best to remove the yellow inserts or paint them over with red lacquer or fingernail polish to discourage bees from stealing the nectar. It is very important not to be tempted to use feeding mixtures containing a red dye, as this may be detrimental to the birds (see this chapter, Question 4: What type of hummingbird feeder is best?).

Question 4: What type of hummingbird feeder is best?

Answer: The more important question is what kind of hummingbird feeder is easiest to keep clean. There are fancy feeders with decorative trim, but most of these are hard to clean. The best feeder is one that you can easily take apart, wash with hot water, and rinse thoroughly, because a sugar solution left in a feeder outdoors for extended periods, especially in hot weather, begins to mold. Mold appears as tiny black dots on the sides of the bottle or as small black masses floating in the fluid. If you see this, you need to rinse out all parts of the feeder with a mild solution of chlorine bleach, and rinse them thoroughly again with water before refilling the feeder. Whatever type of feeder you choose, you should flush it out with hot water once a week (soap or cleaner is not necessary), and if it is very hot outside, you may want to clean it twice a week or more, because the nectar can ferment in hot weather. As a rule, if you believe the solution in your feeder is not good enough for *you* to drink, it is time to change the nectar. You can use a bottle brush to scrub the inside, and every month you should soak your feeder for about an hour in a solution of a quarter-cup of bleach to a gallon of water (or one-half ounce of bleach per quart of water).

Hummingbird biologists prefer two types of feeders: the upside-down bottle over a plastic base, and the flying saucer feeder that is flat with a shallow solution container below the ports (see figure 26). Both types have a plastic feeding platform, usually red, and multiple feeding ports that consist of holes about one-eighth inch in diameter. The holes allow the bird to probe into the lower part of the feeder to access the sugar solution. If you use an upside-down bottle feeder, tighten the bottle only enough to keep the feeder from leaking. If you screw it too tightly, you may break the plastic. The sun will fade the red surface over time, but the birds will continue to come to the feeder, as they have learned it is a source of nectar.

Some feeders have bee guards made of thin rubber stretched across the feeder port with an X cut into the rubber. The bird can probe through the X but bees cannot. The flying saucer feeders are made so that the solution is separated from the top plate by enough space to prevent bees from reaching the sugar solution. In feeders built with upside-down bottles and plastic bottoms, the solution runs up to the rim of the feeder port where bees can easily feed, and bees will attempt to feed unless there is a bee guard or they are otherwise discouraged (see this chapter, Question 8: How can I discourage insects and animals from visiting my feeder?). There are also feeders with a single

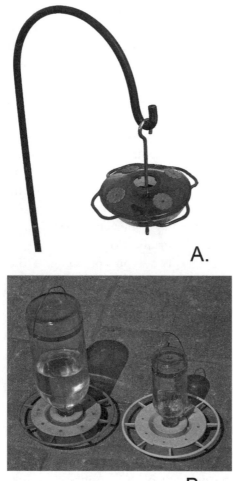

Figure 26. Preferred hummingbird feeders: *A*, satellite or flying-saucer feeder comes apart, the red plastic top separating from the clear plastic nectar reservoir, making this feeder easy to clean; *B*, two sizes of the upside-down bottle feeder. When the bottle is unscrewed, the red plastic base separates into two parts for easy cleaning.

A.

B.

port. The bottle hangs upside-down and usually has a stopper in the opening that is fitted with a bent tube made of clear plastic or glass. When the feeder is hanging, the bent tube is at about a forty-five degree angle to the ground, allowing the birds to feed while hovering in their familiar head-up position.

Multiple-port feeders are more fun to watch, because once there are many birds in the area they will all come around the feeder at the same time. Interestingly, there is usually no territorial aggression and the birds seem to share the feeder ports well, providing you with a good opportunity to watch a number of birds hovering with tails spread, making identification a bit easier.

Question 5: How do I make nectar to put in my hummingbird feeder?

Answer: We suggest that you take the time to make your own nectar rather than purchasing a mix at the store. Most of the mixes contain a red dye powder that manufacturers use to sell the mix to people who believe that red will attract hummingbirds. We'll say it again: hummingbirds will come to any food source once they locate it, just as they will come to a flower of any color once they learn that it will provide nectar. Some scientists are concerned that the red dye in commercial mixes may cause tongue lesions in hummingbirds, although that has not been conclusively demonstrated. But just to be safe, please spread the word—no nectar mix with red dye.

Making a nectar solution is simple, and it can be stored in the refrigerator in a clean glass or plastic container from which it is easy to pour. The formula is four parts water to one part sugar. For example, for five cups of solution, start with a clean saucepan that will hold at least five cups of water. Measure four cups of clean tap water into the pan. If you are using tap water that is heavily chlorinated, boil the water for a few moments so the chlorine will evaporate. If your water is purified or charcoal filtered, just heat the water until it is warm and then add one cup of plain granulated sugar. Do not use any other form of sweetener such as honey, artificial sweetener, powdered sugar, or brown sugar because the sugars or chemicals in these products are difficult, if not impossible, for the bird to digest, and their use can sometimes result in fungus infections.

Stir the sugar into the water until it is completely dissolved, then take the pan off the stove and let the mixture cool to room temperature. Hummingbirds will drink nectar that is more or less concentrated than the proportion we recommend, but we know from experience and from the nectar chemistry of plants preferred by hummingbirds that this concentration is within the range they prefer. Too high a concentration attracts honey bees to the feeder. Too low a concentration encourages the birds to go to someone else's feeder where they can find a four-to-one solution. There is no need to fill the feeder full if there aren't many birds around. The sugar solution will stay fresh in your refrigerator for two to three weeks.

Question 6: Where is the best place to hang my hummingbird feeder?

Answer: A feeder needs to be hung in a safe place (see Chapter 6, Question 1: What are the natural predators of hummingbirds?). A feeder can be suspended from the eaves of a roof to hang right outside a window, as long as there is no windowsill from which a predator can reach the feeder. It can be hung from a tree branch, from a bracket mounted on a pole or on the side of your house, or from a purchased metal pole with a hook made specifically to hold hummingbird feeders. Hanging a feeder in the sun is no problem if there is shade nearby. Most birds like to have vegetation relatively near the feeder (within ten to twenty feet) so they can quickly fly to cover if a predator suddenly appears.

If you live in the western United States and hang more than one feeder, you may increase the number of hummingbird species that visit, as well as the total number of birds, according to Alona Bachi, hummingbird biologist from the University of Arizona. Single territorial male hummingbirds, especially Anna's Hummingbird *Calypte anna,* will try to defend all feeders in an area, but once the number of other birds increases to a threshold where the male cannot keep track of all the feeders, he will give up, and many birds can then feed from any and all feeders with little competition. In areas where birds gather prior to migration or on a migration route, many feeders can be hung near each other because the volume of birds is so high that the only competition arises among individuals trying to access the same feeding port.

Question 7: How does a hummingbird find my feeder?

Answer: If you live in an area where hummingbirds are known to be present, hummingbirds will find your feeder by sight in the same way that they find nectar-bearing flowers. Once a hummingbird has located your feeder and found it to be a good source of nutrition, other hummingbirds will follow. Researchers suspect that there is no communication among hummingbirds about the location of the new nectar source as there is among honey bees, but birds watch their neighbors and fly to see what they have discovered. If you have no flowering plants and there are no nectar sources in your neighborhood, it may take a long time before hummingbirds locate your feeder. But if there is any nectar in the area, they will eventually find your feeder.

We have found that a feeder hanging on a pole in a backyard in a new subdivision, where there was no vegetation within one-quarter mile, attracted a hummingbird in a few days. The birds are much more common in most places than you might expect. They fly long distances looking for nectar sources, and one is likely to fly over your yard, spot that bright red plastic feeder base, and stop by to see if it is of any interest. Based on banding results, some hummingbirds fly more than fifty miles a day from their home base in search of nectar. Don't be discouraged—just keep the feeder fluid fresh and they will come.

Question 8: How can I discourage insects and animals from visiting my feeder?

Answer: The problem of keeping unwanted guests away from hummingbird feeders has been around for a long time and has never been completely solved. Here are some things you can try to keep specific animals away.

Ants have to climb up to the feeder, so you can interrupt their route. If your feeder is hanging from a pole stuck in the ground (the commercial ones look like a shepherd's crook) and isolated from touching anything else, you can smear a little bit of a sticky substance around the pole near its base. Ants cannot cross the sticky barrier. One product used is Tanglefoot, a sticky goo used to discourage pigeons from nesting on city buildings. If you are concerned that a bird or small mammal may get stuck in the goo, make a hole in the bottom of a plastic drinking cup the same diameter as the pole. Turn the cup upside-down and slide it up the pole from the bottom. Secure a small pipe clamp or wrap some tape around the pole a foot or so off the ground to keep the cup from sliding down, then smear Tanglefoot inside the cup. Now ants cannot cross the sticky barrier and birds cannot get caught, as the goo is up inside the cup.

If your feeder is hung from a tree branch or the eave of your house, you need a different method to prevent ants from reaching it. Wild-bird stores sell ant guards, a cup with a hook on the open end and a hook on the bottom. If you fill the cup with water and hang it on the line coming down from the branch or eave, then hang the feeder from the hook on the bottom of the cup, ants cannot cross the watery moat. However, unless you live in a high-humidity climate, the water will quickly evaporate and the guard will need to be refilled. You could fill the guard with oil that will not evaporate, but a bird might try to feed on the oil and become ill. A safe alternative is to turn the ant guard upside down and smear Tanglefoot inside the cup.

Bees collect sugar to make honey, and the more concentrated the sugar solution, the better the bees like it. One way to discourage bees from your feeders is to offer them an alternative source of the high concentration of sugar they like. Fill an old coffee can or other large tin can half way with a solution of one part sugar to two parts water. Stand half a dozen sticks in the can that reach above the mouth of the can. The bees will walk down the sticks and drink the sugar solution. An alternate method is to fill a separate hummingbird feeder with the same highly concentrated mixture—the bees will go there instead of to your other feeders. In *Why Do Bees Buzz?* authors Elizabeth Capaldi Evans and Carol A. Butler describe several experiments that have demonstrated the preference of honey bees for higher concentrations of sugar than hummingbirds favor. Once the

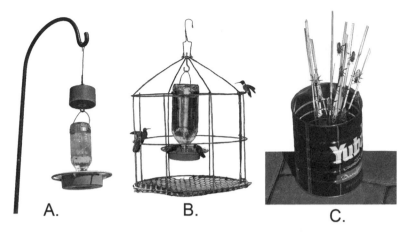

Figure 27. Discouraging unwanted visitors: *A*, commercially available ant guard with the open end facing down. A thin ring of Tanglefoot around the upper inside keeps ants from crawling down to your feeder; *B*, wire bat guard keeps nectar-feeding bats from draining your feeder at night; *C*, can filled with concentrated sugar solution and sticks attracts honey bees away from your feeder.

hive locates this rich source of sugar, they will ignore your hummingbird feeder with the weaker concentration.

Another way to discourage bees is to lightly spray the areas around the feeding ports of your hummingbird feeder with an aerosol cooking spray like Pam; sometimes garlic-flavored Pam works best, but any type will do. The bees do not like to get their feet in the oily substance and the hummingbirds don't touch it or even seem to notice it, since they do not land on those surfaces.

Nectar-feeding bats are common in the southwestern United States and throughout Mexico and the tropics. Since these bats feed at night, you can avoid having them drink all your feeders dry by bringing the feeders inside in the evening and hanging them back up in the morning. An alternative is to construct a bat guard to hang around your feeder. The bat guard is a cylinder made of wire fencing with wire squares of about four to six inches. Cut a section of fencing about twenty-four inches high and fifty to sixty inches long and roll it into a cylinder about fifteen to twenty inches in diameter. Fasten the ends together and then clip the two uppermost horizontal wires away, leaving the vertical wires standing up. To hang the bat guard, bend these vertical wires together and fasten them to a coat-hanger hook, or make a hook of wire. Use the bottom end of the same wire to form a hook to receive the holder of your hummingbird feeder. Next, run three or four wires across the open bottom of the guard or cover the bottom with mesh to prevent bats from flying up from below.

Nectar-feeding bats have a large wingspan and cannot fly through the openings in the guard. They cannot hover outside the guard and reach the feeder ports even with their long tongues, and we have never seen them hang onto the wires. Hummingbirds have no problem with the guard, using it as a temporary perch and flying through the openings with ease. This guard also excludes most avian predators and other predators such as athletic felines.

Bears are less likely to be a concern, but in the western United States and Canada, black bears can be a problem. The bears love to tear the plastic bottom off bottle feeders and drink the sugar water. There are two solutions to this problem. The first is the easiest: since most bear problems occur at night, just take the feeders down in the evening and put them back up in the morning, when you know bears are not in the area. Otherwise you will have to hang the feeders higher than the tallest bear can reach. Hanging the feeder on a long wire from an overhead tree limb or constructing a post with a cross-arm high in the air often works, but this means having either to rig a pulley system to get the feeder down so you can refill it or to use a long-handled hook to reach it.

Birds of some species may appreciate the opportunity to drink from your feeder, since they naturally eat fruit and fruit juice and feed on flower nectar in the wild. Chief among these potential visitors in the United States are orioles and woodpeckers. Most people enjoy watching orioles at a feeder, but woodpeckers tend to be heavier and may tip the feeder, often causing the fluid to spill. They also stay at the feeder for a long time and drink lots of solution. Since they cannot hover, you can try to discourage them by purchasing feeders without the usual ring of perches around the perimeter of the feeder base, but then the hummingbirds will have to hover in order to drink. Other small birds such as warblers, finches, and other species will also occasionally sample your sugar solution. They will not drink much since they usually cannot easily reach the solution because the ports are too small for their bills and their tongues are not long enough. Most of us just put up with the woodpeckers, enjoy their antics, and keep a supply of sugar solution on hand.

Other animals that may try to reach your feeders are ring-tailed cats in the southwestern United States and Mexico, and possibly raccoons and coatimundi. Ring-tailed cats can climb any post or tree and slide down wires to reach the feeder, but raccoons and coatis are perhaps not as skillful. Again, these marauders are active at night, so bringing your feeders in just before dark is the only solution. Squirrels have the ingenuity to access almost any seed feeder, but we have not seen them pay any attention to a hummingbird feeder.

Question 9: Will my feeder interfere with hummingbirds' natural impulse to migrate?

Answer: Contrary to popular belief, you will not keep hummingbirds from migrating in the fall by leaving your feeder out. Hummingbirds will leave when they are ready, but the cues they use to begin their migration have not yet been determined. (See Chapter 5, Question 3: What tells a hummingbird when to migrate?)

Question 10: Will a hummingbird return to my feeder the following year?

Answer: If an adult hummingbird survives the winter, it is highly probable that it will return to its breeding location the following spring. Juveniles that may have fed at your feeder before migrating south will probably go to a nearby area to set up their own nesting and feeding territories. We know from banding returns that hummingbirds are faithful in using the same feeder on migration stops and on breeding territories (see Chapter 2, Question 1: Are hummingbirds intelligent?).

EIGHT

Identifying and Photographing

Question 1: What is the best way to identify hummingbirds?

Answer: Knowing the names of the hummingbirds you are watching can increase the enjoyment of observing them and may lead you to ask questions and learn more about the species in the area. If you are living in or visiting the United States or Canada, your task is far easier because there are only around twenty common species in North America (see table 1). In Mexico, Central America, or South America there are hundreds of species and identification can be much more difficult.

The males of most species are so colorful that it is relatively easy to identify them if you can get a good view for long enough to remember or write down their color patterns. In about 30 percent of hummingbird species there is no sexual dimorphism, that is, the sexes look alike externally. There are some species in which both sexes are drab (most hermits and a few trochilids), without bright colors or conspicuous patterns, and for these you will have to take note of the size, shape, and color of the bird's bill, as well as less conspicuous differences in plumage color and patterns.

Several general bird identification guides that include hummingbirds and a few that specialize in hummingbirds have been published in North America. We recommend the hummingbird guides by Steve Howell and Sheri Williamson (see appendix D). A good field guide should include the resident hummingbirds with

Table 1. Hummingbird Species Documented in North America

Species	Relative abundance north of Mexico	Locations where most birds have been documented*	Habitat
Green Violet-ear	Accidental	Mexico; TX, AR	Woodlands
Green-breasted Mango	Accidental	Mexico; TX	Forest edge
Cuban Emerald	Accidental	Cuba; FL	Woodlands
Broad-billed	Common	Mexico; AZ, NM, TX, LA, CA	Woodlands
White-eared	Rare	Mexico; AZ, NM, TX	Coniferous forest
Xantus's	Accidental	Baja CA; CA	Desert scrub
Berylline	Rare	Mexico; AZ, TX	Woodlands
Buff-bellied	Common	Mexico; TX, LA, MS, AL, FL	Coastal tropical forest
Cinnamon	Accidental	Mexico; AZ, NM	Coastal scrub
Violet-crowned	Uncommon	Mexico; AZ, NM, TX, CA	Sycamore forest
Blue-throated	Common	Mexico; AZ, NM, TX, CO	Mountain riparian forest
Magnificent	Common	Mexico; AZ, NM, TX, CO	Woodlands
Plain-capped Starthroat	Rare	Mexico; AZ	Desert scrub
Lucifer	Uncommon	Mexico; AZ, NM, TX	Dry woodlands
Bahama Woodstar	Accidental	Bahamas; FL	Open woodlands
Ruby-throated	Abundant	All of eastern US west to prairies, north to southern Canada; Mexico	Deciduous forest

Table 1 Hummingbird Species Documented in North America, *continued*

Species	Relative abundance north of Mexico	Locations where most birds have been documented*	Habitat
Black-chinned	Abundant	Western US east to prairies, north to BC, Canada; Mexico	Deciduous woodlands
Anna's	Common	Mexico; CA, AZ, NM, OR	Coastal scrub to mountain forest
Costa's	Common	Mexico; CA, AZ, NM, TX, NV	Desert scrub
Calliope	Common	BC and AB, Canada, WA, ID, MT, WY, CA, UT, NV, AZ, NM, TX; Mexico	Coniferous forest
Bumblebee	Accidental	Mexico; AZ	Mountain coniferous forest
Broad-tailed	Common	ID, MT, NV, WY, CO, AZ, NM, TX; Mexico	Mountain coniferous forest
Rufous	Common	Southern AK through BC and AB, Canada; WA, OR, ID, CA, AZ, NM, TX, Gulf Coast; Mexico	Coastal rain forest
Allen's	Common	CA, AZ, Gulf Coast; Mexico	Coastal, riparian

1998 Check-list of North American Birds. 7th ed. and updates through 2009. Washington, D.C.: American Ornithologists Union.
* There are hundreds of scattered records of wandering birds not listed in this table.

a map of their geographic range, show male and female of each species, and offer short descriptions of their plumage, of how they differ from similar species, of their voice, and of the habitat where they are most likely to be found. If you are interested in more detail, see the species accounts in the *Birds of North America* series listed in appendix D. Each account devotes twenty pages or more to summarizing what is known about one species, with tables and graphs and descriptions instead of photographs.

Question 2: What features distinguish one hummingbird species from another?

Answer: Characteristics to note when trying to identify hummingbirds include length and color of bill (upper and lower

Figure 28. The back of the head of a juvenile male Black-chinned Hummingbird *Archilochus alexandri,* showing the pale tips of each feather that create a scaly appearance when viewed from a distance. These buff-back feathers gradually wear away in the fall.

mandible), color of gorget (throat), color of crown, color of breast and flanks, and shape and pattern of tail (color of each tail feather, including the presence of white at their tips). Remember that the color of the iridescent feathers in the gorget changes with the angle of light and your viewing angle (Chapter 3, Question 8: What are iridescent feathers?). The true color of an iridescent patch appears when the sun is behind you and the bird is facing you.

In the fall, you will find adults together with young birds that have hatched in the summer. The youngsters start out with plumage that closely resembles the adult female's, and without the bird in your hand so you can closely examine its tail or wing or look for corrugations on the bill, you will not be able to distinguish an adult female from a juvenile bird. One juvenile plumage characteristic you might see with binoculars is buff back (see figure 28). Each feather of the crown of the head and down the back of the bird has a light gray-to-rusty thin, buff- colored margin. These light-colored margins wear off within weeks, but while they are present, they give juvenile birds a somewhat scaly appearance.

Question 3: How can I tell a male from a female hummingbird?

Answer: About 70 percent of hummingbird species are sexually dimorphic, meaning males look different from females, and in these cases it is easy to tell the difference between male and female adults. Males usually have more colorful and iridescent plumage than females do, and a crest or a long or unusually shaped tail will be present or exaggerated in males. Males of almost all the common North American species have a brilliantly colored iridescent gorget (throat) that is lacking in most females. The male Ruby-throated Hummingbird, common in the eastern United States, has a brilliant red gorget that shades into black on the chin, while the male Black-chinned Hummingbird common throughout the western states has a solid black gorget and a bright violet collar below the black chin. Males of other species have blue, red, green, violet, purple, rose, or orange gorgets.

In some species, particularly in the hermit subfamily, there are no plumage differences or other external sexually distinguishing features. For these monomorphic species, the only way to tell the difference between male and female in the field is to watch their behavior. Females may be building nests, incubating eggs, or feeding the young, and males usually make impressive courtship displays by flying (see Chapter 4, Question 1: How does a hummingbird attract a mate?). Males are more aggressive, driving competitors away from their feeding territory, and females can be seen performing aggressive displays to defend their nest.

Sexing juvenile birds in late summer is difficult because young of both sexes frequently resemble the adult female. Although there are some minor differences in feather shapes and patterns, these are usually difficult to see unless the bird is in your hand. As fall approaches in North America, the juvenile males of many species begin to develop the colored gorget of

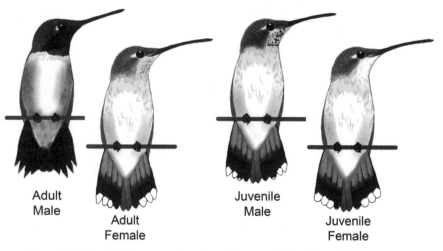

Adult
Male
    Adult
    Female

Juvenile
Male
    Juvenile
    Female

Figure 29. The dark gorget makes the adult male Black-chinned Hummingbird *Archilochus alexandri* easy to identify. Although the birds in the other three images look alike, the adult female Black-chinned Hummingbird has a long and slightly down-curved bill, a lightly marked throat, and an outer tail feather pointed at the tip. The juvenile male has some black and/or some violet in the gorget, and the outer tail feather is pointed. The juvenile female looks like the adult female but has a rounded, not pointed, outer tail feather.

the adult. In some species, adult females also have colored gorget feathers that partially cover the throat, and this can confuse the attempt to sex female and juvenile hummingbirds. You can learn to tell the sex of most juveniles in the fall by using an advanced identification guide. When the birds return in the spring, most will be in their full adult plumage.

Question 4: Where are the best places to see hummingbirds in the wild?

Answer: In southern Arizona and Mexico, where hummingbirds are plentiful, many bird lovers put out feeders to attract the birds. Places where feeders are visible to the public are well-known in the local area—just ask around or consult the local bird-finding guidebook. Some places even have benches and shaded areas for visitors and may provide field guides so you can identify the birds as they come to the feeders, but carrying your own field guide for the area is appropriate. In southeastern Arizona, which has the highest hummingbird species diversity in the United States, there are a number of public viewing areas. With a little digging you can find excellent sites in Central and South America and in the Caribbean where birdwatchers are welcome. Remember that hummingbirds are found only in the Americas, so there is no point in looking for them in the south of France, for example, even though it seems like perfect hummingbird country. See appendix B for a list of some exhibits and gardens where you can see hummingbirds.

Of course, the best place to see hummingbirds is on your own property if you live in an area where hummingbirds visit (see Chapter 7 for information about setting out and maintaining a feeder so hummingbirds will come to you).

Question 5: Why don't people keep caged hummingbirds as pets?

Answer: With their combination of beauty and small size, hummingbirds would seem at first glance to be suitable to be kept as pets in cages, singly or in pairs, like parakeets or canaries. Because of their ability to hover, it would even seem that they, unlike other birds, could adequately exercise their wings in a relatively small cage. But there are several reasons why this is not possible, tempting though it may be.

The overarching reason in the United States is that it is illegal. Hummingbirds are protected by the United Nations Convention on International Trade of Endangered Species (CITES). Species are listed that are not necessarily threatened with extinction but that are at risk unless trading is strictly regulated. Twenty-three hummingbird species are listed under the Migratory Bird Treaty Act, and the birds are covered under other treaties, including the Wild Bird Conservation Act. It is illegal to keep any wild bird in captivity without a permit, because removing a bird from the wild is equivalent to killing it in terms of maintaining the species' population. Indiscriminate killing of birds such as Passenger Pigeons, Carolina Parakeets, and Great Auks has led to their extinction, and unregulated trapping and trade in hummingbirds could have the same result. This is compounded by the fact that hummingbirds do not readily breed in captivity, so their removal from the wild results in an overall population decline.

Hummingbirds are not social birds and they can be very aggressive and territorial, easily becoming stressed in confined surroundings. In the United States, the only places they are successfully kept in captivity are in a handful of exhibits that are spacious and elaborate enough to replicate their environment in the wild so well that they even nest and breed within the enclosures. The Arizona-Sonora Desert Museum and the San Diego Wild Animal Park report consistent success with breeding and maintaining healthy hummingbirds.

The only books about keeping hummingbirds in captivity were written by two Europeans who kept large numbers of hummingbirds in their private collections, and they report success with captive breeding after much trial and error. A. J. Mobbs in Great Britain in the early 1980s and Walter Scheithauer in Germany in the early 1960s discuss the details of their care of the birds, and Mobbs even discusses how best to transport the birds when traveling to exhibit them. A contemporary Netherlands breeder, Jack Roovers, has an elaborate web site where he discusses his success in breeding the birds.

Inspired by their accounts, an American, Wayne Schmidt, writes on his web site about his unsuccessful attempts to get permission to import hummingbirds, not as pets (although he admits he thinks they might have great potential as pets) but for a private facility that he hoped to operate, "dedicated to breeding them with the intention of giving the offspring to zoos." After many years without success, in 1982 he obtained written permission from the U.S. Fish and Wildlife Service to capture a native Anna's Hummingbird *Calypte anna* for a brief period of time in order to study its behavior in captivity. He trapped the bird in the wild, using a wire cage containing a feeder so that the bird could be trapped without being touched. He reports that the bird spent much of its flying time with its head pressed against the cage's roof (a typical reaction of a hummingbird under stress), but otherwise the bird fed and perched in what appeared to be a normal manner. Schmidt released the bird after less than one hour, and it apparently was not seriously traumatized since he reports that it continued to come to his feeders for many months.

Question 6: Why are there so few hummingbird exhibits in zoos and museums?

Answer: Compared with the number of live butterfly exhibits in the world (almost two hundred are listed in coauthor Carol A. Butler's book, *Do Butterflies Bite?*), few zoos or museums have live hummingbird exhibits (for some of the difficulties involved in keeping hummingbirds in captivity, see this chapter, Question 5: Why don't people keep caged hummingbirds as pets?). A few facilities that are open to the public have gardens with feeders and plantings designed to attract wild hummingbirds, and in some of these facilities hummingbirds and butterflies share the same space. In the few very successful exhibits, the birds nest and breed and young birds are raised to adulthood in the aviary. The locations we have confirmed in the United States and

Europe are listed in appendix B, but you may find others if you inquire as you travel.

To obtain hummingbirds from other countries for an exhibit in the United States requires an import permit from the U.S. Fish and Wildlife Service and export permits from the birds' country of origin. Permission is also required from the Service to house captured local species in conjunction with research, as well as to keep birds that are obtained from other zoos that have a surplus due to a successful breeding program (and in Europe from private breeders). Injured wild birds that have recovered in the care of a certified rehabilitator may also become part of an exhibit.

Very little written information is available for a zoo or museum interested in establishing a hummingbird aviary. A how-to manual about maintaining hummingbirds in an exhibit in the United States was published in 2002 and updated in 2004 by representatives of three of the most successful exhibits in the United States: Karen Krebbs of the Arizona-Sonora Desert Museum, David Rimlinger of the San Diego Zoo, and Michael Mace of the San Diego Wild Animal Park. An online version of their *Hummingbird Husbandry Manual* is available. Exhibitors in Europe use the Dutch Hummingbird Foundation as a resource, and their first husbandry manual was published in 2006 by the European Association of Zoos and Aquaria (EAZA). The *EAZA Husbandry Guidelines* were compiled by Linda Roest of Inholland College and Joost Lammers, curator of Birdpark Avifauna in the Netherlands.

The husbandry manuals offer lots of specific information. For example, the U.S. manual discusses how to carry hummingbirds on an airplane, recommending that you check your luggage and keep the birds in a box on your lap, sitting by the window to get the most light. Keeping each bird in a mesh bag, you should take them out to feed them every forty-five minutes. They describe what is needed to set up a successful exhibit, including how much space should be provided for each bird so they are not overcrowded and will be inclined to set up territories and nests. They also discuss, among many topics, how to transition wild birds to a packaged diet containing carbohydrates, protein, fat, vitamins, and minerals; the importance of cleanliness and of using chemical-free water; and the pros and cons of raising your own fruit flies. A healthy hummingbird can eat hundreds of fruit flies a day, so this last point is an important issue. Other than these two manuals, there is almost no published information about caring for hummingbirds in captivity.

What seems to be the primary difficulty in maintaining a live hummingbird exhibit, once the basics are in place, is that the birds are not likely to survive if they become injured or ill. The EAZA guidelines were requested because of the interest from European zoos in exhibiting hummingbirds and "the devastating short lives they've lived in zoos in the past," as the manual explains. Based on information in the International Species Information System, the authors followed up on fifty-three Amazilia Hummingbirds *Amazilia amazilia* that were listed as being kept in different zoos, and they found that that most of the birds had died after from one to ten months in captivity. The U.S. manual puts it this way: "When many hummingbird species exhibit signs of illness they are already declining, and efforts to improve their condition may not help. Also, the veterinary care and medication for hummingbirds has not been perfected for such a small-sized bird."

In a personal communication, Ken Reininger, curator of birds at the North Carolina Zoo, explained that there are several special challenges to veterinary diagnosis and treatment because of the small size of the birds. If a hummingbird becomes ill, its size makes it difficult to restrain for a proper examination. It is virtually impossible to collect a blood sample for diagnostic purposes because of the bird's small blood volume. And if there is medication that might be helpful, it can be administered only by diluting it in a nectar feeder. Ensuring the proper dosage is almost impossible, because a sick bird may have a depressed appetite. Also, the bird's extremely small bones are almost impossible to splint or repair. A veterinarian can sometimes wrap a broken wing but risks damaging the flight feathers in the process, compromising the bird's ability to fly until the feathers grow back. Common injuries like a broken wing or a head injury from flying into glass or into a wall can be quite serious, and if the bird does not recover quickly, such injuries often lead to decline and death. Once a bird is unable to fly and feed itself, it is likely to injure itself further and become debilitated.

Murray Fowler, former chief of the zoological medical service at the University of California, Davis, includes a few pages about hummingbirds in his 2001 book on medicine and surgery for South American wild animals. He briefly mentions administering an anesthetic in a facemask for a hummingbird, but that does not seem to be a common practice.

In our discussion of migration, we describe the process by which hummingbirds accumulate stored fat to fuel their migratory flights (Chapter 5, Question 2: How are hummingbirds able to fly so far?). They are able to efficiently make use of the fat by transferring it to the liver, where it is converted into fatty acids that can be metabolized to meet the body's need for energy during a long migratory flight. Fowler points out that in a confined space, lack of exercise may result in an excessive accumulation of fat (obesity), as well as inhibited liver function (hepatic lipidosis). These conditions may be reversed if lower caloric intake can be arranged and more space can be provided to encourage additional exercise (sounds like an all-too-familiar human problem).

Although torpor is normal for wild birds as a way to conserve energy, it may be a sign of illness or stress in a captive hummingbird when a bird nods its head excessively or appears sleepy (see Chapter 2, Question 11: How do hummingbirds conserve energy?). It is also not a good sign if a bird constantly fluffs its feathers when the other birds in the area seem comfortable (fluffing when it is cold and windy is normal to provide increased insulation). Harassment by other birds can be stressful as well, and it is a sign of stress when a bird flies back and forth repeatedly, hangs on to the exhibit wire, or persistently seeks to escape from the aviary.

Tapeworms in the small intestine are common in birds that eat arthropods (insects). Many birds seem to live normal lives for years with a significant intestinal infestation of tapeworms, which is discovered only upon necropsy. According to the U.S. manual, birds at Arizona-Sonora Desert Museum are not treated for tapeworms because there is no current protocol. The EAZA manual mentions a treatment for tapeworms that is available from Jack Roovers, the Dutch breeder who has been successful raising hummingbirds in captivity (see this chapter, Question 5: Why don't people keep caged hummingbirds as pets?).

Fungus in the bird's throat as a result of a bad batch of food or due to a bird's being immune-compromised because of stressful conditions is another problem (see Chapter 6, Question 3: Do hummingbirds get sick?), but this condition seems to be treatable, with a good response evident in one or two days. Ken Reininger confirmed that oral or systemic fungal infections are the only illnesses he has consistently had luck treating in his hummingbird exhibit.

Despite all these limitations, a female Black-chinned Hummingbird has been thriving in the collection of the North Carolina Zoo for thirteen years and individuals of several other species have led long, healthy lives in other zoos. The Arizona-Sonora Desert Museum has reported a surplus of birds due to successful breeding in their aviary. While you can enjoy viewing hummingbirds in those few aviaries that support them, it is more instructional and enjoyable to watch them in the wild if you are lucky enough to have access to a garden, or if you visit or live in one of the many places where they regularly occur in large numbers.

Live animal exhibits change from year to year, so to avoid being disappointed, it is always sensible to phone or e-mail in advance to make sure there are hummingbirds present in an exhibit you plan to visit.

Question 7: How can I photograph hummingbirds when they move so fast?

Answer: Most average-sized hummingbirds have a wing-beat rate of forty to fifty times per second when hovering; that's 2,400 to 3,000 times per minute, exceptionally fast by any standard. To freeze this rapid wing motion, photographers must go to great lengths, typically using strobe lights with a duration of 1/10,000 second or less.

For the general photographer, we suggest a digital camera with as high a megapixel count as you can afford (eight megapixels, for example, will produce a relatively sharp image, even after it has been enlarged). If possible, use a camera either with a 10x optical zoom (not digital zoom) or a digital single lens reflex (SLR) that allows you to change lenses. You need a telephoto lens that is three hundred millimeters or greater because the birds are so small, and you usually cannot get very close to them except when they are at a feeder. Most of the high-quality lenses are image stabilized and powerful enough to take good photos of hummingbirds, but they are all expensive. When the camera and lens is handheld, you should use a shutter speed equal to or greater than the length of the lens (for example, if you use a lens of four hundred millimeters, your shutter speed should be 1/400 of a second or faster). The advantage gained from using a tripod is that you can lower the shutter speed when taking a photo of a perched bird and increase the depth of field by closing the aperture (increased f stop). While a flash may be necessary in low-light situations, unless it can flash at about 1/10,000 of a second it will not freeze the wing tips of a hovering hummingbird. Cameras with a built-in flash will not be effective at more than fifteen to twenty feet. High-speed synchronized flash units concentrate much more light on your subject, but if you are taking photographs from more than twenty-five feet, you may need to add a Better Beamer with its Fresnel lens to focus the light on your subjects.

You may be able to stand very near a feeder and wait patiently for a bird to land, or you can put your camera on a tripod and use a remote shutter cable or wireless release and take pictures with your camera relatively close to the feeder but with you at a distance. To be sure you get the entire bird in the photo, you need to use a feeder with only one feeding port so you can aim your camera at the spot where the bird will hover when it feeds.

If you want to try a more elaborate setup, you can place flashes to the sides of the hovering position that are synchronized with the camera's shutter with an infrared beam.

Bird photography is best when there is lots of light and you can set your shutter speed as fast as the available light will allow. The birds are in constant motion, and most of your images will have some blur if the wings are moving. It is easier to get a nice sharp photo if a bird is perched while resting or feeding. When photographing a quietly perched bird, you can lower the shutter speed and increase the f-stop to increase the depth of focus. With a telephoto lens, or when using an optical zoom, the depth of focus is reduced so that only a thin plane is in focus and everything ahead of or behind that plane is fuzzy. By increasing the f-stop (making the camera's opening smaller), this plane becomes thicker, and more of your image will be in focus.

You need to remain still while photographing hummingbirds, because they zoom away if they see any unusual motion nearby. Wear dull-colored clothing instead of white or bright colors. If you are using a telephoto lens, it is a good investment to buy a camouflage cover for it so it will not be so obvious. To reduce stress and camera shake while holding your camera and heavy telephoto lens, it is ideal to use an image-stabilized lens and a monopod or tripod with a free-moving but balanced swivel support to facilitate positioning your camera quickly. And you may want to think about setting up a background in the form of a large board or mat painted with a neutral background color placed behind the feeder.

Make sure to carry an extra battery for the camera and a spare memory card because many, many shots are required to get one good photo. For best results, process your own photos on the computer using a program like Adobe Photoshop.

This all sounds like a lot of effort and expense and that may very well be true, but to get a great photo of one of these remarkable birds is quite rewarding.

NINE

Research and Conservation

Question 1: Are hummingbirds endangered?

Answer: More than 335 species of hummingbirds have been identified and described (see Chapter 1, Question 7: How many species of hummingbirds are there in the world?). Although the Endangered Species Act does not list any hummingbird in the United States as endangered, Birdlife International, an organization that looks at the status of bird species throughout the world, takes the position that forty-eight species, or 14 percent of the family, are critically endangered (nine), endangered (fourteen), near threatened (nineteen), or vulnerable (six). If the destruction and loss of habitat continues at the pace of the past ten years, it is probable that these species will be lost within ten to one hundred years.

A 2008 study by Susan Wethington and Nash Finley of the Hummingbird Monitoring Network identified two major areas where hummingbirds are most threatened: in southern Mexico, and in the Andes Mountains from Ecuador to northern Argentina. Other places where smaller numbers of species are threatened are Cuba, small areas in Central America, eastern Brazil, northern South America, and parts of the Atlantic coast of central South America. Most of these threatened species rely on small ranges of forest habitat that are distributed at altitudes between sea level and over 7,550 feet (2,300 meters). Little is known about their natural history. In the United States and Canada, hummingbirds are protected by the Migratory Bird

Treaty Act of 1918 as amended through 1989. This act implements various treaties and conventions between the United States and Canada, Japan, Mexico, and the former Soviet Union for the protection of migratory birds. The act provides extensive and detailed protection against hunting or possessing the birds, their nests, or their eggs, and against buying, selling, or bartering any product using their parts. Researchers who obtain the proper permits may possess and transport birds as needed for their scientific studies, including bird banding (see this chapter, Question 5: Why do researchers band hummingbirds?). Laws in Central and South America may not be as restrictive.

The use of pesticides puts hummingbirds at risk because they depend on flowers and insects for their survival, both of which pass along the chemical poisons to the birds. Habitat destruction eliminates flowers that some species feed on, and the birds are not always able or willing to switch to another food source. Birds also fly into panes of glass and are injured or die, so the presence of people and development in a hummingbird-rich area endangers them too (see Chapter 6, Question 7: What dangers do hummingbirds face from people?). The current list of threatened and endangered species is available online.

Question 2: Are hummingbirds valuable to the economy?

Answer: Hummingbirds serve as the primary pollinators for approximately 130 species of plants in the western United States, and at least another 20 in the eastern states, as documented by Paul Johnsgard of the University of Nebraska–Lincoln in 1997. Almost 300 species were listed in 2007 by Juan Francisco Ornelas and colleagues at the Instituto de Ecologia, Veracruz, Mexico, as producing nectar used by hummingbirds, and probably many more species in Mexico and Central and South America have not yet been documented. Most of the birds' nectar sources (the flowers hummingbirds pollinate) are wildflowers, but some trees and food plants such as madras thorn *Pithecellobrium dulce* and tamarind *Tamarindus indica* depend on hummingbirds for pollination. The fruit of madras thorn has sweet pulp and can be eaten raw or prepared as a beverage. It has a variety of uses in folk medicine. The tamarind tree produces a fruit in a brown pod with a juicy, sweetly acid pulp that is used as an ingredient in chutneys and curries, and formerly was used in medicines and for preserving fish. It may be eaten raw or diluted in a sweetened beverage. A dye obtained from tamarind leaves has been an article of commerce since medieval times. Hummingbirds also pollinate tabebuia (*Tabebuia aurea*), a tree common from Mexico to northern Argentina and on the Caribbean islands. Its primary use is as a hardwood to make furniture and decking; it has the highest fire rating (A1), the same as concrete, which means it will not burn. The wood is denser than water so it does not float, and the bark is sometimes used medicinally.

Another economic contribution attributable to these unique and attractive birds comes from birders and tourists who visit places to observe the birds and learn about them. Throughout the Americas, especially from southeastern Arizona throughout Mexico, Central, and South America, hummingbirds are the group of birds most sought after by birding tourists.

Around the world, a growing number of public aviaries display hummingbirds in captivity (see appendix B for a list of zoos and museums with hummingbird exhibits), but the most satisfying way to observe them is to travel to an area where they are plentiful and to see them in the wild. Bird-watching is one of the fastest-growing hobbies in the United States, and companies that organize and lead birding tours throughout the world are keeping pace. Birders spend millions of dollars annually on transportation, room and board, and the salaries of trip organizers and leaders.

Question 3: How do researchers capture hummingbirds for study?

Answer: Only an authorized researcher is permitted to capture hummingbirds for banding or study, and there are a few safe techniques they commonly use to capture the birds without

Figure 30. A Hall trap set with the trigger line ready to release the mesh curtain when a bird lands on the feeder. (*Photograph by Carol A. Butler*)

harming them. It is important to minimize stress to the bird and to cause it no physical harm.

The best method we know of is the Hall trap, a collapsible cylindrical trap that can be easily carried and rapidly set up to catch hummingbirds. The trap consists of a firm wire or plastic mesh top and bottom, each about two feet in diameter, and a cloth curtain that forms the sides. The bottom hangs from the top by three lines about eighteen inches long. The weighted cloth curtain, made of a material similar to bridal veil netting, hangs from the edge of the wire mesh top and is raised by lines that lead from the bottom of the curtain through the top of the trap, over a pulley, and then to a trigger line that is held by the trapper several feet away. A feeder is hung in the center of the trap, and when a bird lands on the feeder, the trapper releases the trigger line and the curtain falls, trapping the bird inside. The trapper then lifts the edge of the curtain and catches the bird in his or her hand.

The other types of trap have disadvantages. Wire cage traps can harm a bird that is not immediately removed. Birds fly into the wire cage and try to push their bill and head through the mesh, or they fly against the roof of the cage and usually lose feathers. Mist nets or traps constructed of mist netting—large black nylon fine-mesh nets strung between poles—can be extremely efficient when used in narrow lanes between heavily vegetated areas. Birds must be removed soon after capture, as they are subject to predation and entanglement. It can take a long time and lots of patience to remove a bird from a mist net if you do not do so immediately. Mist nets work well for songbirds and larger species and even for hummingbirds in thick brush locations where the birds cannot see the netting ahead of them, but because hummingbirds have the unique ability to make a sudden stop in midair, hover, back away from the net, and then fly over the top, they can often avoid mist nets set in an open area. Comparisons by the Hummingbird Monitoring Network of the numbers of hummingbirds caught using mist nets and Hall traps in the same area have shown that Hall traps are far more efficient for monitoring populations of hummingbirds.

A Russell trap is a setup of two mist nets, one arranged around poles on three sides of a square and the second used to cover the top. One side is left open for the bird to enter feeders that are hung on poles inside the trap. When a bird lands on a feeder, the trapper rushes into the open side of the trap and the bird flies into the mist netting, where it can be captured immediately.

Once a bird is trapped by one of these methods, it is placed gently into a mesh holding bag. This keeps the bird safe until the researcher can measure and weigh it, and either apply a band or record the number from its existing band (see this chapter, Question 5: Why do researchers band hummingbirds?).

Question 4: What is bird banding?

Answer: Banding, called "ringing" in Europe, is the process of placing a small, uniquely numbered anklet around a bird's leg in order to be able to identify that bird again. The first recorded banding of a bird with a metal band was in about 1595 when King Henry IV of England banded his Peregrine Falcons. When one of his falcons was lost, it was later identified by its band, about 1,350 miles away in Malta.

John James Audubon is credited with the first banding in America, tying silver cords to the legs of a brood of migratory phoebes (insect-eating birds in the tyrant flycatcher family Tyrannidae). When the birds returned the following year, he was able to identify them by the bands. Scientific banding with individually numbered metal bands began in the early 1900s, and a system for collecting banding data was put in place in the United States and Canada in the 1920s.

A bird's wearing a band is equivalent in comfort level and weight to a person's wearing a watch or a bracelet. Accepted standard bird-banding criteria state that the "load" (bands or transmitters) that researchers place on wild flying birds should not exceed 3 to 5 percent of the bird's body weight. A band for an average 3.5 gram hummingbird weighs about 0.001 grams, less than 0.03 percent of the bird's body weight. This is one hundred times less than the suggested standard. The band is usually made of an aluminum alloy, or sometimes of monel or another material that is harder and tougher than aluminum. Larger bands used on raptors, parrots, and seabirds are usually made of harder metals that are resistant to saltwater and are more difficult for the bird to remove. For some birds, the bands have to be locked on with rivets so that the bird cannot remove them. But since hummingbirds are unable to manipulate a band that is around their leg, the band can be very thin and pliable but strong. No lock is needed and the band is curled so that the butt ends meet cleanly.

The bands are issued by the Bird Banding Laboratory (BBL), part of the U.S. Geological Survey, and each band bears a unique number. Because hummingbirds are so small, the five-digit number on each band is preceded by a capital letter; for all other birds, the letter is replaced by a string of three to four numbers because there is more room on the band. All bands except hummingbird bands have a message printed on the inside instructing the finder to report it to the BBL, but hummingbird bands are just too small to carry that message.

Question 5: Why do researchers band hummingbirds?

Answer: Banding allows researchers to identify individual birds with confidence and to learn about their history. It establishes that a bird was at a particular place on a specific day, so recapturing the bird provides information about how long the bird has lived, if and how far it has migrated, and its present condition for future reference.

When hummingbirds are captured as part of a banding project approved by the BBL, each bird is carefully removed from the trap and placed in a soft mesh bag. Proceeding in the order in which the birds were captured, the bander removes a bird from its bag and examines it. A recorder usually assists the bander, noting the location, date, and time, and the detailed information dictated by the bander during the one- to two-minute examination of the bird: species, sex, and life stage; the color of the plumage and shape and pattern of certain feathers for identification purposes; wing, tail, and bill measurements; signs of molt or migratory fat; weight (see figure 31); evidence of an egg within (see figure 32); and any other distinguishing signs of the bird's condition. If the bird is already wearing a band, its number is recorded; if not, a tiny, uniquely numbered band is attached to its tarsus (lower leg) with special banding pliers that keep the band from overlapping. Then the bander refreshes the bird with a drink of nectar and releases it.

Figure 31. Monitoring hummingbirds in Madera Canyon, Arizona: *A*, a piece of soft fiberglass windowscreen holds each hummingbird for weighing after it has been banded and processed. This Magnificent Hummingbird *Eugenes fulgens* weighs about seven grams; *B*, feeding a hummingbird that has been processed and is ready for release. Birds lick up the sugar solution while being lightly held. Most are more interested in feeding than in escaping capture. (*Photographs by Carol A. Butler*)

Coauthor George West has a permit to band hummingbirds and has processed more than fourteen thousand. He is one of about two hundred and fifty trained researchers in the United States and Canada who have a specific research proposal that requires banding hummingbirds. All banders are required to submit banding records annually to the BBL, which stores the records in a master database that is accessible to all researchers.

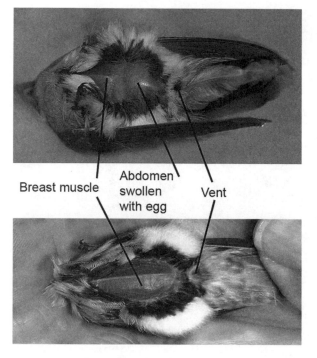

Breast muscle   Abdomen
                 swollen   Vent
                 with egg

Figure 32. Live adult female Black-chinned Hummingbirds *Archilochus alexandri* with the feathers on their abdomens blown aside. *Top,* bird with a developing egg under her belly skin; *bottom,* bird without an egg.

In addition to many private citizens and academic research-ers, qualified employees of state and federal wildlife agencies conducting research on birds are also permitted to band birds. The BBL requires a bander to be specially trained by others already holding permits. A hummingbird bander must have the eyesight, manual dexterity, and knowledge to work with the tiny birds and bands. A bander must be able to safely trap the bird and hold it without causing harm, use the right size band on each species, and be able to identify the bird as to species, age, and sex. In addition, most banders take measurements and make observations, such as if the bird is in molt, if it has any migratory fat, its reproductive status, and whether it is carry-ing pollen (so the source might someday be identified). Even though this sounds like a lot to do, processing a bird usually takes only a few minutes.

Question 6: How can I become qualified to band hummingbirds?

Answer: In order to obtain a permit to band any bird you must have a research program that is acceptable to the Bird Banding Laboratory (BBL), the agency of the U.S. Geological Survey that issues banding permits, and you must be permitted to band by the state in which you wish to do your research. At one time, anyone could get a banding permit to band birds in the backyard, and all that was required was the submission of a banding report at the end of the year. In recent years, however, the BBL has become much more restrictive in the issuing of permits, usually approving them only for persons affiliated with an agency, university, or other organization that has an established ornithological research program or mission.

If you want to band hummingbirds, you must have a need to band them in order to find out something about hummingbirds that you could not learn in any other way. Most of the reasons for banding are related to the ability to identify individual birds. For example, the only way to know the age of a wild bird is to catch the same individual again after it has been banded. To monitor populations of hummingbirds, we learn about the recapture rate of birds banded in prior years by identifying individual birds. Although we can learn where members of a species go when they migrate simply by finding that species in a southern location, we cannot know where the individuals came from without being able to trap birds and examine their bands.

If you are interested in becoming a licensed hummingbird bander, you must train with a bander certified by the BBL. This involves apprenticing at a banding location, learning how to identify all species that might occur at the location and how to determine age and sex of each individual. You learn how to cut and form bands, what size band is appropriate for which bird, and how to apply the band. You also learn how to measure and weigh a bird, record data, feed the bird, and use a computer program to record and submit your information to the BBL annually. Some people do not have the manual dexterity to handle the tiny bands and tiny birds, and some are not careful enough to ensure that the birds would be safe during trapping and handling. To find out where you can learn more about banding birds, talk to a licensed hummingbird bander in your area.

Question 7: What should I do if I see or rescue an injured hummingbird?

Answer: Although as a general rule it is illegal for anyone but a licensed bander or rehabilitator to touch so much as a feather of a hummingbird, anyone is permitted to rescue a bird that is in danger. The U.S. Fish and Wildlife Service amended the regulations governing the handling of migratory birds (50 CFR Part 21) effective November 5, 2007, to allow anyone to remove a hummingbird from a building "in which a bird might pose a threat to themselves, to public health and safety, or to commercial interests." The ruling specifies that the bird "must be captured using a humane method and, in most cases, immediately released into the wild. . . . An exhausted, ill, injured, or orphaned bird must be immediately sent to a rehabilitator."

If you believe a hummingbird is injured or otherwise debilitated and cannot fly, it is safest to gently place the bird in a cloth mesh bag (a knee-high stocking will do) inside a dark box until it can be delivered to a rehabilitator. Contact the nearest rehabilitation facility or veterinarian and ask if they will treat the bird. In the meantime, you can make up a solution of sugar water so you are prepared to give the bird some nourishment (see Chapter 7, Question 5: How do I make nectar to put in my hummingbird feeder?). If the rehabilitation facility advises it, you can dip the tip of the bill into the solution and see if the bird will feed. You can tell it is feeding by watching for pulsations in its throat as its tongue goes in and out as it sips the solution, but often a bird in this situation will not feed.

If you encounter a dead hummingbird—or any dead bird—with a band, you should remove the band (you can open a hummingbird band with your fingernails or small tweezers), flatten it out, copy down the letter and five numbers, and either go on the Web to report the band to the BBL or telephone them toll-free at 1-800-327-BAND to report the information. The BBL will find out where and when the bird was banded, and they will send you a report. The dead bird should go to a licensed bander, who is permitted to donate it to a public scientific or educational institution within six months. Veterinarians are authorized under their license to dispose of dead birds, so if you cannot locate a bander, take the bird to your local veterinarian or animal hospital. Statistics are collected on the deaths of all migratory birds, and these experts are mandated to make the appropriate reports.

Question 8: What can I do to help support the conservation and protection of hummingbird populations?

Answer: If we wish to have hummingbirds in our lives and for future generations to enjoy, we need to make sure they have what they need to reproduce successfully and maintain viable populations. Increased development and cutting of native forests are major threats to the survival of the large variety of hummingbirds throughout the Americas, and while some species of hummingbirds will adapt, it is evident that others will not. Warming climates change the timing of flowering of the plants on which hummingbirds depend for their energy supply, and this disturbs the mutualism that enables the plants and their pollinators to thrive.

To understand these changes and to determine how to improve hummingbirds' ability to survive, it is important to continuously monitor hummingbird populations and the changes in the plant species that provide them with nectar. The Hummingbird Monitoring Network (HMN) tracks the variety and number of hummingbirds at more than thirty sites in the western United States and southern Canada. The HMN is expanding the number of sites in all states from Texas westward and into Mexico. Visit their web site to learn more about the network and about how you can help as a supporter of the program or an assistant at a banding station.

Currently, a broad partnership is developing among nonprofit organizations, universities, and governmental agencies at the federal and state/provincial levels to address conservation and protection issues in the United States, Mexico, and Canada. As new opportunities for participation develop, the HMN web site will be updated to keep everyone informed.

We encourage you to request that your elected representatives work to uphold the current bird protection laws like the Migratory Bird Treaty Act and the Endangered Species Act. Encourage them to support organizations that study populations of hummingbirds to learn where they are most abundant and where they are vulnerable to habitat loss. You can also support organizations that are concerned with setting aside native forests and woodlands for wildlife, as well as trusts and organizations that acquire lands and place them in conservation status (see appendix C for a list of some hummingbird organizations).

Garden Plants That Attract Hummingbirds

There are many flowers that will attract hummingbirds to your garden Most are perennial flowers that are relatively easy to grow and care for, while some are shrubs, climbing vines, or trees. Most of the plants on this list are available from a nursery or garden center. Most entries give the genus but not the species (spp.), because many varieties are available. Ask the gardener or horticulturalist at your local plant nursery which species or varieties are best for your area. Most of the plants listed have flowers in the red family, and these seem the most popular for attracting hummingbirds. Those with yellow and blue flowers are more attractive to butterflies and honey bees.

The first group includes plants most frequently recommended by several web sites and hummingbird-gardening books. For more detailed information, search for "hummingbird flowers" on the Web or consult the books and web sites listed.

Plants Most Frequently Recommended

Bee Balm *Monarda* spp. Annual and perennial; pink to red flowers
Canada Lily *Lilium canadense*. Perennial; pink to red flowers
Cardinal Climber or Cypress Vine *Ipomoea quamoclit*. Annual; pink to red flowers
Cardinal Flower *Lobelia cardinalis*. Perennial; red flowers
Delphinium *Delphinium elatum*. Perennial; magenta, blue, purple flowers
Fuchsia *Fuchsia* spp. Shrub; white, pink, mostly red flowers
Hollyhock *Althea* spp. Perennial; white, pink to red flowers
Honeysuckle *Lonicera* spp. Perennial vine or shrub; white, pink, orange flowers
Hummingbird Trumpet *Zauschneria cana*. Perennial; red flowers

Indian Pink *Spigelia marilandica.* Perennial; red flowers with yellow centers

Mountain Flame *Anisacanthus* spp. Perennial; yellow, orange to red flowers

Mountain Rosebay *Rhododendron catawbiense.* Shrub, pink flowers

Penstemon *Penstemon* spp. Perennial; pink, red to blue flowers

Red Buckeye *Aesculus pavia.* Small tree; orange-red to red flowers

Red Columbine *Aquilegia canadense.* Perennial; red flowers

Rose of Sharon *Hibiscus syriacus.* Large shrub; white, pink, red, lavender to purple flowers

Scarlet Gilia or Skyrocket *Ipomopsis.* Perennial; red flowers

Silk Tree *Albizia julibrissin.* Small tree; puffy pink flowers

Spotted Jewelweed *Impatiens capensis.* Annual; yellow flowers with red spots

Trumpet Creeper or Trumpet Vine *Campsis* or *Bignonia* spp. Annual; yellow to pink and red-orange flowers

Other Hummingbird Attractors

Abelia *Abelia grandiflora.* Shrub; white to pink flowers

African Floxglove *Ceratotheca.* Annual; white, pink to purple flowers

Agastache *Agastache* spp. Perennial; red, pink to blue flowers

Aloe *Aloe karasburgensis.* Perennial; pink to red flowers

Aloe vera *Aloe barbarensis.* Perennial; yellow flowers

Azalea *Rhododendron* spp. Shrub; white, pink to blue and purple flowers

Bottlebrush *Callistemon* spp. Shrub to small tree; red, orange, or white flowers

Bouvardia *Bouvardia glaberrima.* Perennial small shrub; red to orange-red flowers

Butterfly Bush *Buddleia davidii.* Shrub; white, yellow, pink, red, blue flowers

Candelilla *Pedilanthus macrocarpus.* Perennial; red flowers

Canna *Cannas* spp. Perennial lily relative; red, pink, orange flowers

Cardinal Monkey Flower *Mimulus cardinalis.* Perennial; red flowers

Cardinal Vine—See Cardinal Climber

Catnip *Nepeta* spp. Perennial; pale violet flowers

Coral Bean *Erythrina flabelliformis.* Perennial; red flowers

Coral Bells *Heuchera sanguinea.* Perennial; pink to red flowers

Cosmos *Cosmos* spp. Perennial; white, yellow, pink to red flowers

Dahlia *Dahlia* spp. Perennial bulb; white, pink, orange to red flowers

Fairy Duster *Calliandra* spp. Perennial small shrub; red to pink flowers

Flame Acanthus or Bear's Breeches *Acanthus mollis.* Perennial; white to
pink flowers
Flame Vine or Golden Shower *Pyrostegia venusta.* Perennial vine;
orange flowers
Flowering Currant *Ribes sanguineum.* Shrub; pink flowers
Flowering Quince *Chaenomeles* spp. Shrub; pink to red flowers
Four O'Clock *Mirabilis jalapa.* Perennial; pink to magenta flowers
Foxglove *Digitalis* spp. Perennial; pink to magenta flowers
Galvezia *Galvezia juncea.* Perennial; red flowers
Gladiolus *Gladiolus* spp. Perennial bulb; flowers of all colors available
Hesperaloe *Hesperaloe* spp. Perennial; white to pink flowers
Iris *Iris* spp. Perennial bulb; most colors available
Jacobiana *Cochliostema jacobiana.* Perennial bulb; pink, red to blue
flowers
Jasmine *Jasminum* spp. Shrub; white flowers
Lantana *Lantana* spp. Perennial shrub or herbaceous; pink, magenta,
yellow flowers
Lilac *Syringa* spp. Perennial shrub; pink to violet flowers
Lobelia *Lobelia laxiflora.* Perennial; red flowers
Lupine *Lupinus* spp. Perennial; pink to blue and purple flowers
Mallow *Malva* spp. Perennial; pink, white flowers
Manzanita *Arctostaphylos* spp. Shrub to small tree; tiny white to pink
flowers
Milkweed or Butterfly Weed *Asclepias tuberose.* Perennial; orange-red
flowers
Mimosa *Mimosa* spp. Shrub to tree; yellow or pink flowers
Monkeyflower *Mimulus hybridus.* Perennial; orange and yellow flowers
Montbretia *Crocosmia* spp. Perennial bulb; vermilion flowers
Morning Glory *Ipomoea* spp. Perennial vine; white, blue, purple, pink,
red flowers
Mountain Garland *Clarkia elegans.* Annual; pink, red, orange, white to
blue flowers
Nasturtium *Tropaeolum majus.* Annual; yellow to orange-red flowers
Petunia *Petunia hybrida.* Annual; white, pink, red, to purple flowers
Rosary Vine *Ceropegia woodii.* Perennial vine; pink flowers
Rose Campion *Lychnis* spp. Perennial; red, pink, white, orange flowers
Sage *Salvia* spp. Perennial to small bush; pink, red to blue flowers
Scarlet Runner *Phaseolus coccineus.* Vine; red-orange flowers
Shrimp Plant *Justicia brandegeana.* Perennial; yellow to orange-red
flowers
Snapdragon *Antirrhinum* spp. Annual; all colors available

Snapdragon Vine *Maurandya antirrhiniflora.* Perennial; blue to red flowers

Speedwell *Veronica* spp. Annual or perennial, pink to blue flowers

Spider Flower *Cleome hasslerana.* Annual; white, pink to red flowers

Touch-me-not *Impatiens* spp. Annual and perennial; all colors available

Trumpet Honeysuckle *Lonicera sempervirens*—See Honeysuckle

Tuberous Begonia *Begonia* spp. Annual; white, pink, orange, red to magenta flowers

Turks Cap *Malvaviscus arboreus.* Perennial; pink to red flowers

Verbena *Verbena* spp. Annual; pink to purple flowers

Water-willow *Justicia* spp. Perennial; orange, pink, red to purple flowers

Weigela *Weigela rosea.* Shrub; pink flowers

Wild Lilac *Ceanothus griseus.* Shrub; white, blue to purple flowers

Zinnia *Zinnia* spp. Annual and perennial; yellow to orange, red flowers

More information is available from these sources:

Arizona-Sonora Desert Museum. *Hummingbirds in Your Garden: How to Attract and Maintain Hummingbirds in your Garden or Patio.* 6-page brochure

Cunningham, V. 2004. *The Gardener's Hummingbird Book.* Minnetonka, Minn.: National Home Gardening Club.

Gates, L., and T. Gates. 2008. *Enjoying Hummingbirds.* Mechanicsburg, Pa.: Stackpole Books.

Stokes, D., and L. Stokes. 1989. *The Hummingbird Book.* Boston: Little, Brown.

www.birdwatchers.com/debtips.htmlwww.dianeseeds.com/flowers/hummingbirds.html

www.hummingbirdworld.com/h/gardens.htm

www.landscaping.about.com/cs/forthebirds/a/hummingbirds.htm

www.thegardenhelper.com/hummingbird.html

www.wild-bird-watching.com/Attracting_Hummingbirds.html

Some Places to See Live Hummingbirds in Exhibits or Gardens

United States

Arizona-Sonora Desert Museum
2021 N. Kinney Road
Tucson, Arizona 85743–8918
http://www.desertmuseum.org/
Tel: 520.883.1380
E-mail: info@desertmuseum.org

Baltimore National Zoo
Druid Hill Park
Baltimore, Maryland 21217
http://www.marylandzoo.org
Tel: 410.396.7102

Beatty's Miller Canyon Guest Ranch
2173 E. Miller Canyon Road
Hereford, Arizona 85615–9667
http://www.beattysguestranch.com/
Tel: 520.378.2728

Butterfly World, Florida
3600 West Sample Road
Coconut Creek, Florida 33073
http://www.butterflyworld.com
Tel: 954.977.4400
E-mail: gardens@butterflyworld.com

Cameron Zoological Park
1701 North Fourth Street
Waco, Texas 76707
http://www.cameronparkzoo.com
Tel: 254.750.8400

Dallas World Aquarium
1801 N. Griffin Street
Dallas, Texas 75202
http://www.dwazoo.com/default.html
Tel: 214.720.2224

Detroit Zoo
8450 W. 10 Mile Road
Royal Oak, Michigan 48067
http://www.detroitzoo.org
Tel: 248.541.5717 ext. 3128

The Living Desert
47–900 Portola Avenue
Palm Desert, California 92260
http://www.livingdesert.org
Tel: 760.346.5694

Madera Canyon
Chuparosa Inn
1300 S. Madera Canyon Road
Green Valley, Arizona 85614
http://www.chuparosainn.com
Tel: 520.393.7370

Madera Canyon
Madera Kubo Cabins
1259 S. Madera Canyon Road
Green Valley, Arizona 85614
Tel: 520.625.2908

Madera Canyon
Santa Rita Lodge
1217 S. Madera Canyon Road
Green Valley, Arizona 85614

http://www.santaritalodge.com/
Tel: 520.625.8746

Marion Paton's Birders Haven Hummingbird Garden
Blue Haven Road
Patagonia, Arizona 85624
Note: ask in the area for directions.

Miami Metrozoo
12400 SW 152nd Street
Miami, Florida 33177–1402
http://www.miamimetrozoo.com
Tel: 305.251.0400
E-mail: eeric@miamidade.gov

Moody Gardens
One Hope Boulevard
Galveston, Texas 77554
http://www.moodygardens.com
Tel: 800.582.4673

North Carolina Zoological Park
4401 Zoo Parkway
Asheboro, North Carolina 27205–1425
http://www.nczoo.org
Tel: 336.879.7000
E-mail: info@ncmail.net

Omaha's Henry Doorly Zoo
3701 S. Tenth Street
Omaha, Nebraska 68107–2200
http://www.omahazoo.com
Tel: 402.733.8401

Ramsey Canyon Preserve
The Nature Conservancy
27 Ramsey Canyon Road
Hereford, AZ 85615
http://www.nature.org/wherewework/northamerica/states/arizona/
    preserves/art1973.html
Tel: 520.378.2785

San Diego Wild Animal Park
15500 San Pasqual Valley Road
Escondido, California 92027–7017
http://www.sandiegozoo.org/wap/location.html
Tel: 760.747.8702

San Diego Zoo
2920 Zoo Drive in Balboa Park
San Diego, California 92112–0551
http://www.sandiegozoo.org
Tel: 619.231.1515

Smithsonian National Zoological Park Pollinarium
3001 Connecticut Avenue NW
Washington, D.C. 20008
http://www.nationalzoo.si.edu
Tel: 212.633.4800

International

Denmark
Copenhagen Zoo
Zoologisk Have
Roskildevej 38
2000 Frederiksberg
http://www.zoo.dk
Tel: +45 72 200 200

England
Zoological Society of London
London Zoo
Regent's Park
London NW1 4RY
http://www.zsl.org
Tel: 020 7722 3333
E-mail: editor@zsl.org

Germany
Zoological Garden Wuppertal
Hubertusallee 30, 42117
Wuppertal.
http://www.zoo-wuppertal.de

Tel: 0049 202 27470
E-mail: kontakt@zoo-wuppertal.de

The Netherlands
Artis Royal Zoo
P.O. Box 20164
1000 HD Amsterdam
http://www.artis.nl/international/index.html
Tel: +31 20 5233400.
E-mail: info@artis.nl

Burgers' Zoo
Antoon van Hooffplein 1
6816 SH Arnhem
http://burgerszoo.nl.colo2.netmasters06.netmasters.nl/index.cfm
Tel: +31 26 442 45 34
E-mail: info@burgerszoo.nl

Vogelpark Avifauna
Hoorn 65
P.O. Box 31
2400 AA Alphen a/d Rijn
http://www.avifauna.nl
Tel: +31 172 487575

Zoo Emmen / Dierenpark Emmen
Hoofdstraat 18
7811 EP Emmen
http://www.dierenparkemmen.nl
Tel: +31 591 850850
E-mail: info@zoo-emmen.nl

Hummingbird Organizations

American Bird Conservancy
1250 Twenty-fourth Street NW, Suite 400
Washington, D.C. 20037
http://www.abcbirds.org
Tel: 202.778.9666

American Birding Association
P.O. Box 6599
Colorado Springs, Colorado 80934
http://www.americanbirding.org
Tel: 719.578.9703

Hummer/Bird Study Group
P.O. Box 250
Clay, Alabama 35048
http://www.hummingbirdsplus.org
Tel: 205.681.2888
E-mail: hummerBSG@aol.com

Hummingbird Monitoring Network
P.O. Box 115
Patagonia, Arizona 85624
http://http://www.hummonnet.org
E-mail: swething@dakotacom.net

The Hummingbird Society
P.O. Box 519
Sedona, Arizona 86324
http://www.hummingbirdsociety.org
Tel: 800.529.3699

Humnet
http://www.museum.lsu.edu/~Remsen/HUMNETintro.html

National Audubon Society
700 Broadway
New York, New York 10003
http://www.audubon.org
Tel: 212.979.3000

National Wildlife Federation
8925 Leesburg Pike
Vienna, Virginia 22184
http://www.nwf.org
Tel: 703.790.4000

The Ontario Hummingbird Project
c/o Cindy Cartwright
4379 Bruce Road 3, RR 3
Saugeen Shores, NOH 2C7
http://www.ontariohummingbirds.ca
E-mail: hummingbirds@bmts.com

Operation Ruby-Throat
Hilton Pond Center for Piedmont Natural History
York, South Carolina 29745
http://www.rubythroat.org
Tel: 803.684.5852
E-mail: education@hiltonpond.org

Recommended Reading and Web Sites

General reading

Gates, L., and T. Gates. 2008. *Enjoying Hummingbirds in the Wild and in Your Yard*. Mechanicsburg, Pa.: Stackpole Books.

Sayre, J., and A. Sayre. 1996. *Hummingbirds: The Sun Catchers*. Minocqua, Wis.: NorthWord Press.

Stokes, D., and L. Stokes. 1989. *The Hummingbird Book*. New York: Little, Brown.

Thurston, H. 1999. *The World of the Hummingbird*. San Francisco: Sierra Club Books.

Readings about Specific Species

(Note: All entries are part of the *Birds of North America* series published in Philadelphia by the Academy of Natural Sciences. Each is a pamphlet of twelve to thirty-two pages.)

Baltosser, W. H., and S. M. Russell. 2000. *Black-chinned Hummingbird (Archilochus alexandri)*. No. 495.

Baltosser, W. H., and P. E. Scott. 1996. *Costa's Hummingbird (Calypte costae)*. No. 251.

Calder, W. A. 1993. *Rufous Hummingbird (Selasphorus rufus)*. No. 53.

Calder, W. A., and L. L. Calder. 1992. *Broad-tailed Hummingbird (Selasphorus platycercus)*. No. 16.

———. 1994. *Calliope Hummingbird (Stellula calliope)*. No. 135.

Chavez-Ramirez, F., and A. Moreno-Valdez. 1999. *Buff-bellied Hummingbird (Amazilia yucatanensis)*. No. 388.

Howell, C.A., and S.N.G. Howell. 2000. *Xantus's Hummingbird (Hylocharis xantusii)*. No. 554.

Mitchell, D. E. 2000. *Allen's Hummingbird (Selasphorus sasin)*. No. 501.

Powers, D. R. 1996. *Magnificent Hummingbird* (*Eugenes fulgens*). No. 221.

Powers, D. R., and S. M. Wethington. 1999. *Broad-billed Hummingbird* (*Cynanthus latirostris*). No. 430.

Robinson, T. R., R. R. Sargent, and M. B. Sargent. 1996. *Ruby-throated Hummingbird* (*Archilochus colubris*). No. 204.

Russell, S. M. 1996. *Anna's Hummingbird* (*Calypte anna*). No. 226.

Scott, P. E. 1994. *Lucifer Hummingbird* (*Calothorax lucifer*). No. 134.

Wethington, S. M. 2002. *Violet-crowned Hummingbird* (*Amazilia violiceps*). No. 688.

Williamson, S. L. 2000. *Blue-throated Hummingbird.* (*Lampornis clemenciae*). No. 531.

Useful Web Sites, Most with Links to Other Resources

Birding the Americas Trip Report and Planning Repository, www.birdingtheamericas.com

Hummer/Bird Study Group, www.hummingbirdsplus.org

Hummingbird Monitoring Network, www.HumMonNet.org

Hummingbird Search Engine, www.whatbird.com

Hummingbird Society, www.hummingbirdsociety.org

Hummingbird Web, www.hummingbirdworld.com/h/resource.htm

Hummingbird World, www.hummingbirdworld.com

Hummingbirds.net, www.hummingbirds.net

Operation Ruby-throat, www.rubythroat.org

Southeast Arizona Bird Observatory, www.sabo.org/hummers.htm

References

Chapter One: Hummingbird Basics

Question 1: What is a hummingbird?

del Hoyo, J., A. Elliott, and J. Sargatal. 1999. *Handbook of the Birds of the World*. Vol. 5, *Barn-owls to Hummingbirds*. Rockville Center, N.Y.: Lynx Edicions.

Grant, V. 1994. Historical development of ornithology in the western North American flora. *Proceedings of the National Academy of Sciences* 91:10407–10411.

Question 3: Where in the world are hummingbirds found?

Berlin, R, 1982. Floral biology, hummingbird pollination and fruit production of trumpet creeper (*Campsis radicans*, Bignoniaceae). *American Journal of Botany* 69:122–134.

Bleiweiss, R., J. A. Kirsch, and J. C. Matheus. 1997. DNA hybridization evidence for the principal lineages of hummingbirds (Aves: Trochilidae). *Molecular Biology and Evolution* 14:325–343.

Gould, J. 1991. *John Gould's Hummingbirds*. Edison, N.J.: Booksales.

Grant, V. 1994. Historical development of ornithology in the western North American flora. *Proceedings of the National Academy of Sciences* 91:10407–10411.

Pleasants, J. M., and N. M. Waser. 1985. Bumblebee foraging at a "hummingbird" flower: reward economics and floral choice. *American Midland Naturalist* 114:283–291.

Tripp, E. A., and P. S. Manos. 2008. Is floral specialization an evolutionary dead-end? pollination system transitions in Ruella (Acanthaceae). *Evolution* 62:1712–1737.

Question 4: When did hummingbirds evolve?

Altshuler, D. L., and R. Dudley. 2002. The ecological and evolutionary interface of hummingbird flight physiology. *Journal of Experimental Biology* 205:2325–2336.

Bleiweiss, R. 1998a. Tempo and mode of hummingbird evolution. *Biological Journal of the Linnean Society* 65:63–76.

———. 1998b. Origin of hummingbird faunas. *Biological Journal of the Linnean Society* 65:77–97.

Bochenski, Z., and Z. M. Bochenski. 2008. An Old World hummingbird from the Oligocene: A new fossil from Polish Carpathians. *Journal of Ornithology* 149:211–216.

Bradshaw, H. D., and D. W. Schemske. 2003. Allele substitution at a flower colour locus produces a pollinator shift in Monkeyflowers. *Nature* 426:176–178.

Garcia-Moreno, J., et al. 2005. Local origin and diversification among *Lampornis* hummingbirds: a Mesoamerican taxon. *Molecular Phylogenetics and Evolution* 38:488–498.

Grant, V. 1994. Historical development of ornithophily in the western North American flora. *Proceedings of the National Academy of Sciences* 91:10407–10411.

Johnsgard, P. A., 1997. *The Hummingbirds of North America*. Washington, D.C.: Smithsonian Institution Press.

Louchart, A., et al. 2008. Hummingbird with modern feathering: an exceptionally well-preserved Oligocene fossil from southern France. *Naturwissenschaften* 95:171–175.

Mayr, G. 2004. Old World fossil record of modern-type hummingbirds. *Science* 304:861–864.

McGuire, J. A., et al. 2009. A higher-level taxonomy for hummingbirds. *Journal of Ornithology* 150:155–165.

Thurston, H. 1999. *The World of the Hummingbird*. San Francisco: Sierra Club Books.

Question 5: How are hummingbirds classified?

1998 Check-list of North American Birds. 7th ed. Washington, D.C.: American Ornithologists' Union.

Clements, J. F. 2000. *Birds of the World, a Checklist*. Vista, Calif.: Ibis.

del Hoyo, J., A. Elliott, and J. Sargatal. 1999. *Handbook of the Birds of the World*. Vol. 5, *Barn-owls to Hummingbirds*. Rockville Center, N.Y.: Lynx Edicions.

Hackett, S. J., et al. 2008. A phylogenomic study of birds reveals their evolutionary history. *Science* 320:1763–1768.

Sibley, C. G., and B. L. Monroe Jr. 1990. *Distribution and Taxonomy of Birds of the World*. New Haven, Conn.: Yale University Press.

Question 6: What are the differences between typical or trochilid hummingbirds and hermits?

del Hoyo, J., A. Elliott, and J. Sargatal. 1999. *Handbook of the Birds of the World*. Vol. 5, *Barn-owls to Hummingbirds*. Rockville Center, N.Y.: Lynx Edicions.

Question 8: How long do hummingbirds live?

Hummingbird Monitoring Network. Protecting the Fog Forest of western Ecuador. http://www.hummonnet.org/preservation/projects .html. Accessed October 6, 2008.

Operation Ruby Throat. Hummingbird-banding results. http://www .rubythroat.org/HummerResultsMain.html. Accessed October 6, 2008.

Wethington, S. 2008. Personal communication (new record for Magnificent at eleven years).

Wethington, S. M., et al. 2002. Longevity records for North American hummingbirds. *North American Bird Bander* 27:131–133.

Question 9: Which are the smallest and largest hummingbirds?

Altshuler, D. L., R. Dudley, and J. A. McGuire. 2004. Resolution of a paradox. Hummingbird flight at high elevation does not come without a cost. *Proceedings of the National Academy of Sciences* 101: 17731–17736.

Gregory, T. R., et al. 2009. The smallest avian genomes are found in hummingbirds. *Proceedings of the Royal Society B: Biological Sciences* 276:3753–3757.

McGuire, J. A., et al. 2009. A higher-level taxonomy for hummingbirds. *Journal of Ornithology* 150:155–165.

Chapter Two: Systems and Senses

Question 1: Are hummingbirds intelligent?

Iwaniuk, A. N., and D.R.W. Wylie. 2007. Neural specialization for hovering in hummingbirds: hypertrophy of the pretectal nucleus lentiformis mesencephali. *Journal of Comparative Neurology* 500:211–221.

Reiner, A. 2008. Avian evolution: from Darwin's finches to a new way of thinking about avian forebrain organization and behavioural capabilities. *Biology Letters* 5:122–124.

Question 2: What do hummingbirds eat?

Blem, C. R., et al. 2000. Rufous Hummingbird sucrose preference: precision of selection varies with concentration. *Condor* 102:235–238.

Collins, B. 2008. Nectar intake and foraging efficiency: responses of honeyeaters and hummingbirds to variations in floral environments. *Auk* 125:574–587.

Johnsgard, P. A. 1997. *The Hummingbirds of North America,* Washington, D.C.: Smithsonian Institution Press.

Powers, D. R., and T. M. Conley. 1994. Field metabolic rate and food consumption of two sympatric hummingbird species in southeastern Arizona. *Condor* 96:141–150.

Roberts, W. M. 1995. Hummingbird licking behavior and the energetics of nectar feeding. *Auk* 112:456–463.

Stiles, F.G. 1995. Behavioral, ecological and morphological correlates of foraging for arthropods by hummingbirds of a tropical wet forest. *Condor* 97:853–878.

Stiles, F. G., and C. E. Freeman. 1993. Patterns in floral nectar characteristics of some bird-visited plant species from Costa Rica. *Biotropica* 25:191–205.

Question 3. Why do hummingbirds need to eat so much?

Powers, D. R., and T. M. Conley. 1994. Field metabolic rate and food consumption of two sympatric hummingbird species in southeastern Arizona. *Condor* 96:141–150.

West, G. C., 1968. Bioenergetics of captive Willow Ptarmigan under natural conditions. *Ecology* 49:1035–1045.

Question 4: How do hummingbirds know which flowers have nectar?

Gill, F. B. 1988. Trapline foraging by hermit hummingbirds: competition for an undefended, renewable resource. *Ecology* 69:1933–1942.

Gonzales-Gomez, P., and R. A. Vasquez. 2006. A field study of spatial memory in Green-backed Firecrown hummingbirds (*Sephanoides sephanoides*). *Ethology* 112:790–795.

Healy, S., and Hurly, T. A. 2006. Hummingbirds. *Current Biology* 16: R392-R393.

Irwin, R. E. 2000. Hummingbird avoidance of nectar-robbed plants: spatial location or visual cues. *Oikos* 91:499–506.

Question 5: How do hummingbirds digest their food?

Johnsgard, P. A. 1997. *The Hummingbirds of North America.* Washington, D.C.: Smithsonian Institution Press.

Powers, D. R., and T. M. Conley. 1994. Field metabolic rate and food consumption of two sympatric hummingbird species in southeastern Arizona. *Condor* 96:141–150.

Roberts, W. M. 1995. Hummingbird licking behavior and the energetics of nectar feeding. *Auk* 112:456–463.

Tilford, T. 2000. *The World of Hummingbirds*. Chicago, Thunder Bay Press.

True, D. 1993. *Hummingbirds of North America*. Albuquerque: University of New Mexico Press.

Verbeek, N.A.M. 1971. Hummingbirds feeding on sand. *Condor* 73:112–113.

Wheeler, T. G. 1980. Experiments in feeding behavior of the Anna Hummingbird. *Wilson Bulletin* 92:58–62.

Question 6: How do hummingbirds get rid of the water from all the nectar they drink?

Bakken, B. H., et al. 2004. Hummingbirds arrest their kidneys at night: Diel variation in glomerular filtration rate in *Selasphorus platycercus*. *Journal of Experimental Biology* 207:4383–4391.

Bakken, B. H., and P. Sabat. 2006. Gastrointestinal and renal responses to water intake in the Green-backed Firecrown (*Sephanoides sephanoides*), a South American hummingbird. *American Journal of Physiology: Regulatory, Integrative, and Comparative Physiology* 291:R830-R836.

Weathers, W. W., and F. G. Stiles. 1989. Energetics and water balance in free-living tropical hummingbirds. *Condor* 91:324–331.

Question 7: Why do hummingbirds have such long bills?

Chalcoff, V., M. A. Aizen, and L. Galetto. 2008. Sugar preferences of the Green-backed Firecrown hummingbird (*Sephanoides sephanoides*): a field experiment. Auk 125:60–66.

Matinos del Rio, C. 1990. Sugar preferences in hummingbirds: the influence of subtle chemical differences on food choice. *Condor* 92:1022–1030.

McWhorter, T. J., et al. 2006. Hummingbirds rely on both paracellular and carrier-mediated intestinal glucose absorption to fuel high metabolism. *Biology Letters* 2:131–134.

Question 8: How can hummingbirds be so active?

Altshuler, D. L., R. Dudley, and J. A. McGuire. 2004. Resolution of a paradox: hummingbird flight at high elevation does not come without a cost. *Proceedings of the National Academy of Sciences* 101:17731–17736.

Lopez-Calleja, M. V., and F. Bozinovic. 1995. Maximum metabolic rate, thermal insulation and aerobic scope in small-sized Chilean hummingbirds (*Sephanoides sephanoides*). *Auk* 112:1034–1036.

Powers, D. R., and T. McKee. 1994. The effect of food availability on time and energy expenditures of territorial and non-territorial hummingbirds. *Condor* 96:1064–1075.

Welch, K. C., Jr., D. L. Altshuler, and R. K. Suarez. 2007. Oxygen consumption rates in hovering hummingbirds reflect substrate-dependent differences in P/O ratios: carbohydrate as a "premium fuel." *Journal of Experimental Biology* 210:2146–2153.

Witt, C. C., et al. 2008. Evolution of hypoxia resistance in Andean hummingbirds. Paper presented at the 126th meeting of the American Ornithologists' Union, Portland, Ore.

Question 11: How do hummingbirds conserve energy?

Bech, C., et al. 1997. Torpor in three species of Brazilian hummingbirds under semi-natural conditions. *Condor* 99:780–788.

Chai, P., A. C. Chang, and R. Dudley. 1998. Flight thermogenesis and energy conservation in hovering hummingbirds. *Journal of Experimental Biology* 201:963–968.

Davies, H., and C. A. Butler. 2008. *Do Butterflies Bite?* Piscataway, N.J.: Rutgers University Press.

Hainsworth, F. R., and L. L. Wolf. 1970. Regulation of oxygen consumption and body temperature during torpor in a hummingbird, *Eulampis jugularis. Science* 168:368–369.

Schmidt-French, B. A., and C. A. Butler. 2009. *Do Bats Drink Blood?* Piscataway, N.J.: Rutgers University Press.

Smith, W. K., S. W. Roberts, and F. C. Miller. 1974. Calculating the nocturnal energy expenditure of an incubating Anna's Hummingbird. *Condor* 76:176–183.

Question 13: Do hummingbirds have a good sense of smell?

Goldsmith, T., and K. Goldsmith. 1982. Sense of smell in the Black-chinned Hummingbird. *Condor* 84:237–238.

Ioale, P., and F. Papi. 1989. Olfactory bulb size, odor discrimination and magnetic insensitivity in hummingbirds. *Physiology and Behavior* 45:995–999.

Kessler, D., K. Gase, and I. T. Baldwin. 2008. Field experiments with transformed plants reveal the sense of floral scents. *Science* 321:1200–1202.

Raguso, R. A. 2008. The "invisible hand" of floral chemistry. *Science* 321:1163–1164.

Steiger, S. S., et al. 2008. Avian olfactory receptor gene repertoires: evidence for a well-developed sense of smell in birds? *Proceedings of the Royal Society B: Biological Sciences* 275:2309–2317.

Question 14: Do hummingbirds hear well?

Lohr, B., and R. J. Dooling. 2004. Hearing in the ruby-throated hummingbird (*Archilochus colubris:* Trochilidae). Paper presented at the Association for Research in Otolaryngology, Daytona Beach, Fla.

Pytte, C., M. Ficken, and A. Moiseff. 2004. Ultrasonic singing by the blue-throated hummingbird: a comparison between production and perception. *Journal of Comparative Physiology* 190:665–673.

Question 15: Do hummingbirds have good eyesight?

Goldsmith, T. H. 1980. Hummingbirds see near ultraviolet light. *Science* 207:786–788.

Question 16: Do hummingbirds hum?

Clark, C. J. 2008a. Fluttering wing feathers produce the flight sounds of male streamertail hummingbirds. *Biology Letters* 4:341–344.

———. 2008b. Anna's Hummingbird chirps with its tail during display dives. *Science Daily.* www.sciencedaily.com/releases/2008/. Accessed October 6, 2008.

Hunter, T. 2008. On the role of wing sounds in hummingbird communication. *Auk* 125:532–541.

Question 17: Do hummingbirds sing?

Ficken, M. S., et al. 2000. Blue-throated Hummingbird song: a pinnacle of non-oscine vocalizations. *Auk* 117:120–128.

Gahr, M. 2000. Neural song control system in hummingbirds. *Journal of Comparative Neurology* 426:182–196.

Ornelas, J. F., C. Gonzales, and J. Uribe. 2002. Complex vocalizations and aerial displays of the Amethyst-throated Hummingbird. *Auk* 119:1141–1149.

Pytte, C. L., M. S. Ficken, and A. Moiseff. 2004. Ultrasonic singing by the blue-throated hummingbird: a comparison between production and perception. *Journal of Comparative Physiology A: Neuroethology, Sensory, Neural, and Behavioral Physiology* 190:665–673.

Pytte, C. L., K. M. Rusch, and M. S. Ficken. 2003. Regulation of vocal amplitude by the blue-throated hummingbird, *Lampornis clemenciae. Animal Behavior* 66:703–710.

Rusch, K. M., C. L. Pytte, and M. S. Ficken. 1996. Organization of agonistic vocalizations in Black-chinned Hummingbirds. *Condor* 98:557–566.

Williams, B., and A. Houtman. 2008. Song of Costa's Hummingbird *Calypte costae. Auk* 125:663–669.

Chapter Three: Feathers and Bones

Question 1: How fast does a hummingbird beat its wings?

Calder, W., and L. Calder. 1992. *Broad-tailed Hummingbird.* No. 16 in *The Birds of North America,* ed. A. Poole and F. Gill. Philadelphia: American Ornithologists' Union.

Clark, C. J. Courtship dives of Anna's hummingbird offer insights into flight performance limits. *Proceedings of the Royal Society B: Biological Sciences* 276:3047–3052.

Clark, C. J., and R. Dudley. 2009. Flight costs of long, sexually selected tails in hummingbirds. *Proceedings of the Royal Society B: Biological Sciences.* 276:2109–2115.

Gill, F. B. 1985. Hummingbird flight speeds. Auk 102:97–101.

Greenewalt, C. H. 1991. *Hummingbirds.* Rev. ed. New York: Dover Publications.

Powers, D. R. 1996. *Magnificent Hummingbird (Eugenes fulgens).* No. 221 in *The Birds of North America,* ed. A. Poole, P. Stettenheim, and F. Gill. Philadelphia: Academy of Natural Sciences.

Robinson, T., R. Sargent, and M. Sargent. 1996. *Ruby-throated Hummingbird (Archilochus colubris).* No. 204 in *The Birds of North America,* ed. A. Poole, P. Stettenheim, and F. Gill. Philadelphia: Academy of Natural Sciences.

Russell, S. M. 1996. *Anna's Hummingbird (Calypte anna).* No. 226 in *The Birds of North America,* ed. A. Poole, P. Stettenheim, and F. Gill. Philadelphia: Academy of Natural Sciences.

Williamson, S. L. 2000. *Blue-throated Hummingbird (Lampornis clemenciae).* No. 531 in *The Birds of North America,* ed. A. Poole, P. Stettenheim, and F. Gill. Philadelphia: Academy of Natural Sciences.

Question 2: How does a hummingbird hover?

Anitei, S. 2006. The hummingbird's hovering ability comes from its brain. *Nature* 13:50.

Iwaniuk, A. N., and D.R.W. Wylie. 2007. Neural specialization for hovering in hummingbirds: hypertrophy of the pretectal nucleus lentiformis mesencephali. *Journal of Comparative Neurology* 500:211–221.

Kaminski, T. 2008. *Hummingbirds! A Natural History DVD*. Rolling Hills
    Estates, Calif.: Nature Video Classroom.
Physorg.com. Hummingbird flight, an evolutionary marvel. http://
    www.physorg.com/news4688.html. Accessed May 15, 2008.
Warrick, D. R., B. W. Tobalske, and D. R. Powers. 2009. Lift produc-
    tion in the hovering hummingbird. *Proceedings of the Royal Society B:
    Biological Sciences* 276:3747–3752.
Williamson, S. L. 2001. *Peterson Field Guides: Hummingbirds of North
    America*. New York: Houghton Mifflin.

Question 4: How many feathers does a hummingbird have?

Clark, H. L. 1906. The feather tracts of swifts and hummingbirds. *Auk*
    23:68–91.

Question 5: How do birds keep their feathers so smooth and the wing feathers in perfect shape?

Brooke, M., and T. Birkhead. 1991. *The Cambridge Encyclopedia of Orni-
    thology*. New York: Cambridge University Press.

Question 7: Are all hummingbirds brilliantly colored?

Kimball, R. T., and J. D. Ligon. 1999. Evolution of avian plumage
    dichromatism from a proximate perspective. *American Naturalist*
    154:182–193.

Question 8: What are iridescent feathers?

Greenewalt, C. H., W. Brandt, and D. D. Friel. The iridescent colors of
    hummingbird feathers. *Proceedings of the American Philosophical Society*
    104:249–253.

Chapter Four: Reproduction

Question 1: How does a hummingbird attract a mate?

Clark, C. J. Courtship dives of Anna's hummingbird offer insights into
    flight performance limits. *Proceedings of the Royal Society B: Biological
    Sciences* 276:3047–3052.
Gaunt, S.L.L. 1996. Song displays, song dialects, and lek mating
    systems in hummingbirds. *Journal of the Acoustical Society of America*
    99:2532–2574.
Harger, M., and D. Lyon. 1979. Lek of the green hermit. *Ibis*
    122:525–530.
MacDougall-Shackleton, E., and H. Harbison. 1998. Singing behavior
    of lekking Green Hermits. *Condor* 100:149–152.

Pizo, M. A., and W. R. Silva. 2001. The dawn lek of the Swallow-tailed Hummingbird. *Wilson Bulletin* 113:388–397.

Ramjohn, C. L., et al. 2003. Lek mating behavior of the Sooty-capped Hermit (*Phaethornis augusti*) in the Paria Peninsula of Venezuela. *Journal of Field Ornithology* 74:205–320.

Question 2: How do hummingbirds protect their mating territory?

Russell, S. M. 1996. Anna's Hummingbird (*Calypte anna*). No. 226 in *The Birds of North America,* ed. A. Poole and F. Gill. Philadelphia: Academy of Natural Sciences.

Question 5: Can hummingbirds of one species mate with those of another species?

Trochlids.com. Hybridization in hummingbirds. http://www.trochi lids.com/hybrid.html. Accessed October 6, 2008.

Question 7: How many young do hummingbirds have each year?

Baltosser, W. H. 1986. Nesting success and productivity of humming-birds in southwestern New Mexico and. southeastern Arizona. *Wilson Bulletin* 98:353–367.

Question 11: How does a female hummingbird feed herself while incubating eggs?

Baltosser, W. H. 1996. Nest attentiveness in hummingbirds. *Wilson Bulletin* 108:228–245.

Question 12: How does a female hummingbird feed her nestlings and what do they eat?

Carroll, D., and N. Carroll. 2006. *First Flight: A Mother Hummingbird's Story.* Kansas City, Mo.: Andrews McMeel.

Carroll, D., and N. Carroll. 2009. *First Flight: A Mother Hummingbird's Story.* DVD. Las Vegas: Concept Images.

Question 13: How quickly do hummingbirds mature?

Greeney, H. F., et al. 2008. *Nestling growth and plumage development of the Black-chinned Hummingbird (Archilochus alexandri) in southeastern Arizona.* Ecuador: Huitzil.

Mayer, R. 2009. *Hummingbirds: Jewels of the Sky, Joy of Motherhood.* DVD. Tucson, Ariz.: Chief Iron Hoof Video Unlimited.

Chapter Five: Flight and Migration

Question 1: How far can a hummingbird fly?

Calder, W. A. 1993. *Rufous Hummingbird (Selasphorus rufus)*. No. 53 in *Birds of North America*, ed. A. Poole and F. Gill. Philadelphia: Academy of Natural Sciences / Washington, D.C.: American Ornithologists' Union.

Chartier, A. 1998. Twenty-two years of Ruby-throated Hummingbird migration at Holiday Beach Conservation Area, Ontario, Canada. *Ontario Birds* 16:101–110.

Gill, R. E., et al. 2009. Extreme endurance flights by landbirds crossing the Pacific Ocean: ecological corridor rather than barrier? *Proceedings of the Royal Society B: Biological Sciences* 276:447–457.

Robinson, T., R. Sargent, and M. Sargent. 1996. Ruby-throated Hummingbird (*Archilochus colubris*). No. 204 in *The Birds of North America*, ed. A. Poole, P. Stettenheim, and F. Gill. Philadelphia: Academy of Natural Sciences.

Stutchbury, B. J., et al. 2009. Tracking long-distance songbird migration by using geolocators. *Science* 323:896.

Willimont, L. A., S. E. Senner, and L. J. Goodrich. 1988. Fall migration of Ruby-throated Hummingbirds in the northeastern United States. *Wilson Bulletin* 100:482–488.

Question 2: How are hummingbirds able to fly so far?

Fuchs, T., et al. 2006. Daytime naps in night-migrating birds: behavioral adaptation to seasonal sleep deprivation in the Swainson's thrush, *Catharus ustulatus*. *Animal Behavior* 72:951–958.

Hackett, S., et al. 2008. A phylogenomic study of birds reveals their evolutionary history. *Science* 320:1763–1768.

Lasiewski, R. C. 1962. The energetics of migrating hummingbirds. *Condor* 64:324.

Rattenborg, N. C., et al. 2004. Migratory sleeplessness in the white-crowned sparrow (*Zonotrichia leucophrys gambelii*). *PLoS Biology* 2:e212.

Question 3: What tells a hummingbird when to migrate?

Berthold, P., E. Gwinner, and E. Sonnenschein, eds. 2003. *Avian Migration*. New York: Springer.

Farner, D. S. 1950. The annual stimulus for migration. *Condor* 52:104–122.

Gwinner, E. 1977. Circannual rhythms in bird migration. *Annual Review of Ecology and Systematics* 8:381–405.

Helm, B., and E. Gwinner. 2006. Migratory restlessness in an equatorial nonmigratory bird. *PLoS Biology* 4:e110.

Rowan, W. 1925. Relation of light to bird migration and developmental changes. *Nature* 115:494–495.

Wolfson, A., and D. P. Winchester. 1959. Effect of photoperiod on the gonadal cycle in an equatorial bird, *Quelea quelea*. *Nature* 184:1658–1659.

Question 4: How do hummingbirds find their way during migration?

Heyers, D. 2007. MA visual pathway links brain structures active during magnetic compass orientation in migratory birds. *PLoS ONE* 2: e937.

Question 5: Do all hummingbirds migrate?

Moran, J. Linking the breeding and wintering ranges of Rufous Hummingbirds (*Selasphorus rufus*) using stable isotopes. Royal Roads University. http://www.royalroads.ca/research/researchers-and-research/current/moran-rufous-hummingbirds.htm. Accessed February 21, 2009.

Rappole, J. H., and K. Schuchmann. 2003. Ecology and evolution of hummingbird population movements and migration. In *Avian Migration*, ed. P. Berthold, E. Gwinner, and E. Sonnenschein. Berlin: Springer Verlag.

Chapter Six: Dangers and Defenses

Question 1: What are the natural predators of hummingbirds?

Bird Watcher's Digest. Praying mantis makes meal of a hummer. http://www.birdwatchersdigest.com/site/backyardbirds/hummingbirds/mantis-hummer.aspx. Accessed September 14, 2008.

Question 2: How do hummingbirds defend themselves and their food supply?

Greeney, H. F., and S. M. Wethington. In press. Proximity to active *Accipiter* nests reduces nest predation of Black-chinned Hummingbirds. *Wilson Journal of Ornithology*.

Question 3: Do hummingbirds get sick?

Fowler, M. E. 2001. Order Trochiliformes (Hummingbirds). In *Biology, Medicine, and Surgery of South American Wild Animals*, ed. M. E. Fowler and Z. S. Cubas. Ames: Iowa State University Press.

Roest, L., and J. Lammers. 2006. *EAZA Husbandry Guidelines: Hummingbirds*. Alphen a/d Rijn, The Netherlands: Birdpark Avifauna and the Hummingbird Foundation.

Saidenberg, A.B.S., et al. 2007. *Serrata marcescens* infection in a Swallow-tailed Hummingbird. *Journal of Wildlife Diseases* 43: 107–110.

Question 4: Do hummingbirds get parasites?

Clayton, D. H., R. D. Gregory, and R. D. Price. 1992. Comparative ecology of neotropical bird lice (Insecta: Phthiraptera). *Journal of Animal Ecology* 61:781–795.

Hyland, K. E., A. Fain, and A. S. Moorhouse. 1978. Ascidae associated with nasal cavities of Mexican birds (Acarina: Mesostigmata). *Journal of the New York Entomological Society* 86:260–267.

Valkiunas, G., et al. 2004. Additional observations on blood parasites of birds in Costa Rica. *Journal of Wildlife Diseases* 40:555–561.

Question 5: How do flower mites interact with hummingbirds?

Da Cruz, D. D., et al. 2007. The effect of hummingbird flower mites on nectar availability of two sympatric *Heliconia* species in a Brazilian Atlantic forest. *Annals of Botany* 100:581–588.

Garcia-Franco, J., et al. 2001. Hummingbird flower mites and *Tillandsia* spp. (Bromeliaceae): polyphagy in a cloud forest of Veracruz, Mexico. *Biotropica* 33:538–542.

Grigg, R. 2000. Hummingbird hitch-hikers. *Creation Ex Nihilo* 22: 20–22.

Hyland, K. E., A. Fain, and A. S. Moorhouse. 1978. Ascidae associated with the nasal cavities of Mexican birds (Acarina: mesostigmata). *Journal of the New York Entomological Society* 86:260–267.

Kaminski, T. 2008. *Hummingbirds! A Natural History DVD*. Rolling Hills Estates, Calif.: Nature Video Classroom.

Lara, C., and J. F. Ornelas. 2002a. Effects of nectar theft by flower mites on hummingbird behavior and the reproductive success of their host plant, *Moussonia deppeana* (Gesneriaceae). *Oikos* 96:470–480.

———. 2002b. Flower mites and nectar production in six hummingbird-pollinated plants with contrasting flower longevities. *Canadian Journal of Botany* 80:1216–1229.

Schmidt-French, B., and C. A. Butler. 2009. *Do Bats Drink Blood?* Piscataway, N.J.: Rutgers University Press.

Question 6: What dangers do hummingbirds face in the environment?

Bolger, D. T., T. A. Scott, and J. T. Rotenberry. 1997. Breeding bird abundance in an urbanized landscape in coastal Southern California. *Conservation Biology* 11:406–421.

Greenberg, R. C., M. Caballero, and P. Bichier. 1993. Defense of homopteran honeydew by birds in the Mexican highlands and other warm temperate forests. *Oikos* 68:519–524.

Lotz, C. N., C. Martinez del Rio, and S. W. Nicolson. 2003. Hummingbirds pay a high cost for a warm drink. *Journal of Comparative Physiology B: Biochemical, Systematic, and Environmental Biology* 173:455–462.

Chapter Seven: Attracting and Feeding

Question 2: How can I attract hummingbirds to my garden or feeder?

Cunningham, V. 2005. *The Gardener's Hummingbird Book*. Minnetonka, Minn.: National Home Gardening Club.

Newfield, N. L., and B. Nielsen. 1996. *Hummingbird Gardens: Attracting Nature's Jewels to Your Backyard*. New York: Houghton Mifflin.

Williamson, S. 2005. *Attracting and Feeding Hummingbirds*. Neptune City, N.J.: T.F.H. Publications.

Question 6: Where is the best place to hang my hummingbird feeder?

Bachi, A. 2008. Resource-diversity relationship in hummingbirds, the underlying mechanism of aggressive resource neglect, and its application to reconciliation in urban habitats. MS thesis, University of Arizona, Tucson.

Question 8: How can I discourage insects and animals from visiting my feeder?

Capaldi Evans, E., and C. A. Butler. 2009. *Why Do Bees Buzz?* New Brunswick, N.J.: Rutgers University Press.

Chapter Eight: Identifying and Photographing

Question 1: What is the best way to identify hummingbirds?

Howell, S. N. G. 2002. *Hummingbirds of North America: The Photographic Guide*. London and San Diego: Academic Press.

Williamson, S. L. 2001. *Peterson Field Guides: Hummingbirds of North America*. New York: Houghton Mifflin.

Question 4: Where are the best places to see hummingbirds in the wild?

American Birding Association. *A Birder's Guide.* (Series for many areas of the United States where hummingbirds might be found. See recent updates on the American Birding Association web site.) www .abasales.com. Accessed October 7, 2008.

Stevenson, M., ed. 2007. *Finding Birds in Southeast Arizona.* 7th ed. Tucson, Az.: Tucson Audubon Society.

Question 5: Why don't people keep caged hummingbirds as pets?

Mobbs, A. J. 1982. *Hummingbirds.* Surrey, Eng.: Triplegate.

Scheithauer, W. 1967. *Hummingbirds.* Trans. G. Vevers. London: Arthur Barker.

Question 6: Why are there so few hummingbird exhibits in zoos and museums?

Krebbs, K., D. Rimlinger, and M. Mace. 2002. Husbandry guidelines: Apodiformes. Riverbanks.org. http://www.riverbanks.org/subsite/ pact/hummingbirds.pdf. Accessed September 26, 2008.

―――. 2004. *Hummingbird Husbandry Manual.* Silver Spring, Md.: American Zoo and Aquarium Association Pact TAG.

Roest, L., and J. Lammers. 2006. *EAZA Husbandry Guidelines: Hummingbirds.* Alphen a/d Rijn, The Netherlands: Birdpark Avifauna and the Hummingbird Foundation.

Chapter Nine: Research and Conservation

Question 1: Are hummingbirds endangered?

Wethington, S., and N. Finley. 2008. Addressing hummingbird conservation needs: initial assessment of threats to the Trochilidae, the family of hummingbirds. Poster session, Fourth International Partners in Flight Conference. McAllen, Tex. February 13–16.

Question 2: Are hummingbirds valuable to the economy?

Johnsgard, P. A. 1997. *The Hummingbirds of North America,* Washington, D.C.: Smithsonian Institution Press.

Ornelas, J. F., et al. 2007. Phylogenetic analysis of interspecific variation in nectar of hummingbird-visited plants. *Journal of Evolutionary Biology* 20:1904–1917.

Question 3: How do researchers capture hummingbirds for study?

Hummingbird Monitoring Network. Protecting the Fog Forest of western Ecuador. http://www.hummonnet.org/preservation/projects
.html. Accessed October 6, 2008.

Question 4: What is a bird band?

Piaskowski, V., K. Scanlan, and S. Mahler. Bird banding. Zoological Society of Milwaukee. http://www.zoosociety.org/Conservation/
BWB-ASF/Library/BirdBanding.php. Accessed October 26, 2008.

Question 5: Why do researchers band hummingbirds?

Patuxent Wildlife Research Center. Who can band birds? 2003.
http://www.pwrc.usgs.gov/bbl/homepage/whocan.htm. Accessed September 30, 2008.

Question 7: What should I do if I see or rescue an injured hummingbird?

Migratory bird permits: removal of migratory birds from buildings.
2007. *Federal Register Rules and Regulations* 72:193.
Ornelas, J. F., et al. 2007. Phylogenetic analysis of interspecific variation in nectar of hummingbird-visited plants. *Journal of Evolutionary Biology* 20:1904–1917.
U.S. Government Printing Office. Title 50: Wildlife and fisheries.
http://ecfr.gpoaccess.gov/cgi/t/text/text-idx?c=ecfr&sid=1a18f7757
4cedd3dc66604f0bc552dfc&rgn=div5&view=text&node=50:6.0.1.1
.4&idno=50#50:6.0.1.1.4.3.1.1. Accessed September 26, 2008.

Index

Page numbers in italics refer to figures

About the Authors

George C. West, Ph.D., is professor of zoophysiology, emeritus, from the Institute of Arctic Biology, University of Alaska Fairbanks, where he spent twenty-one years training graduate students and studying the physiological adaptations of birds and mammals to the arctic and subarctic. He has been interested in birds since age nine and has sketched and painted birds all his life. After moving to Arizona in 1996 he became interested in hummingbirds and cofounded the Hummingbird Monitoring Network, a nonprofit organization that is working to protect and preserve hummingbirds and their habitats. For the past ten years he has been deeply involved in hummingbird research. At the same time he continues to write about Alaska in his latest revision and update of *A Birder's Guide to Alaska*, published by the American Birding Association. He also provides illustrations for many authors, newsletters, posters, bird guides, brochures, and books. A complete resume and list of publications is available upon request.

Carol A. Butler, Ph.D., is the coauthor of the Rutgers University Press question-and-answer series that includes *Do Butterflies Bite?* (2008), *Do Bats Drink Blood?* (2009), and the forthcoming *Why Do Bees Buzz?* (2010) and *How Fast Does a Falcon Dive?* (2010). She also coauthored *Salt Marshes: A Natural and Unnatural History* (2009) and *The Divorce Mediation Answer Book* (1999). She is a psychoanalyst and a mediator in private practice in New York City, an adjunct assistant professor at New York University, and a docent at the American Museum of Natural History.